THE
REAL
ESTATE
ROOKIE

THE REAL ESTATE *ROOKIE*

*practical advice
for the first-time residential
property investor*

TERESA WAINWRIGHT

CHOICE BOOKS

A CHOICE BOOK
Copyright general text © Teresa Wainwright 2003
First published in 2003 by
CHOICE Books, Australian Consumers' Association
57 Carrington Road Marrickville NSW 2204 Australia
http://www.choice.com.au

Reprinted in 2003 (twice)

National Library of Australia
Cataloguing-in-publication data

Wainwright, Teresa.
The real estate rookie : practical advice for the
first-time residential property investor.

Includes index.
ISBN 1 920705 15 5.

1. Real estate business - Australia. 2. Real estate
investment - Australia. 3. Rental housing - Australia. I.
Title.

332.632430994

Edited by Kathryn Lamberton
Cover design by Howard Binns-McDonald
Internal design and typesetting by Midland Typesetters
Back cover photograph © Roy Wainwright

Printed in Australia by Southwood Press

CONTENTS

This book is dedicated to my husband Roy —
my partner in investment and in life.

ACKNOWLEDGEMENTS

In the six years since I started investing in property,
I have met many real estate professionals. Some of them
have proved particularly helpful and honest, and I would
like to take this opportunity to thank them.

So, Sarah Godwin and Helen Fry, thank you for your
excellent management of our properties.

Thanks, too, to real estate agents Lea Lamacka, Gavin
Langridge and Dawn White, conveyancers Janette Chap-
man and Piera Della Torre, accountant Craig Reeves, and
Sarah Sullivan and Liz Karamoshos who look after all my
banking needs.

Special thanks to Simon Vine and Greg Tabe of Nelson
Wheeler Chartered Accountants, Adelaide, for their dili-
gent checking of the taxation and depreciation facts and
figures quoted in Chapter 10.

Finally, my thanks go to all my case study contributors,
to Richard Smart and Colette Batha at CHOICE Books,
and to my editor Kathryn Lamberton.

DISCLAIMER

Every effort has been made to ensure that the content of this book is accurate. However, while the information contained herein was current at the time of writing, it should be noted that the facts and figures may be superseded at any time. All advice is intended as a general guide only.

Readers are encouraged to seek independent advice from qualified financial professionals before embarking on any investment strategy.

Neither the author nor any other party contributing to this book, including the publisher, may be held responsible for any action or claim resulting from the use of this book or any information contained herein.

ROOKIE (noun)
A person who is new to an organisation or an activity
Cambridge International Dictionary of English

INTRODUCTION

Every day I meet people, good hard-working people, who dream of going on overseas holidays, putting their children through university, buying a decent car, or maybe retiring early, but cannot, because they do not have sufficient money.

These people have jobs and, in most cases, are paying off mortgages on their own homes. Unfortunately, they do not realise that *all* the things they wish for are possible in the future if they start building a wealth base *now*.

Once people find out that I have a number of investment properties, they usually want to know how they can achieve the same. They see that I am just an average person holding down a job, not so different from them, and yet I am well on the way to financial independence.

I have advised a number of potential investors, all of whom have gone on to purchase their first investment property. Of all the investors I have helped (one started only two years ago and has already bought their third investment property), the overriding concern has *not* been about obtaining finance or the taxation benefits of owning an investment property.

What they all want to know is what kind of property they should buy. What sort of property is going to rent easily? How can they minimise their risk?

Existing books, even the bestsellers, gloss over the type of property to purchase and concentrate almost exclusively on the financial aspects of the investment.

So it seemed clear to me that the market needed a step-by-step, 'paint by numbers' type of book that novice, or rookie, investors could follow and be assured of success. With that in mind I wrote *The Real Estate Rookie — practical advice for the first-time residential property investor*.

The Real Estate Rookie is *unique* in that it includes interviews not only with existing investors, but also with tenants. For the first time, the would-be investor is advised on the most desirable features of a property *by the people who will be renting it*. Written for investors with little or no experience in real estate, it is a clear, down-to-earth guide for anyone who has ever thought about investing in residential real estate but didn't know where to start.

Chapter 1

WHO INVESTS, WHO RENTS?

How many rock stars do you know? What about movie stars, famous artists or top authors? Your answer is likely to be none. Such occupations are seen by many as lucrative and glamorous, and the people who enjoy such careers as a lucky minority in our society. Real estate investment, too, is seen as a glamorous, out of the ordinary way of making money, but unlike singers, actors, artists and writers, you do not need a natural talent to become a successful investor — you can learn this skill. In fact, if you do your research and buy wisely, it is relatively easy to become rich and successful through property investment. I am constantly amazed that more people do not take up the challenge.

So in purchasing this book you have taken a positive step towards changing your financial future for the better, and believe me, you will thank yourself for it in years to come.

Studies by the Australian Bureau of Statistics[1] (all available at www.abs.gov.au) show that the private residential rental market provides around 26 per cent of housing for Australian households, and 74 per cent of that accommodation is provided by private landlords — people like you and me (ABS 1301.01, Survey of Income and Housing Costs, 1999–2000).

1. ABS data used with permission from the Australian Bureau of Statistics

In just over five years I have amassed a property port-folio which puts me in the top group of all investors — those who own 10 properties or more — and it has cost me only a bit of my time and a few dollars each week. You can do the same.

If I do nothing more than sit back and let my tenants pay off my debts I will own all my assets outright in less than 20 years.

What will *you* own if you sit back and do nothing?

Profile of an average investor
People invest for all sorts of reasons.

Many people are *accidental* investors. Some may be lucky enough to inherit a property. Single people meet other single people and decide to move in together. If they both already own their own homes, this can leave them with one spare property. Sometimes the end of a marriage can leave one partner with a property that no longer suits their needs. In each case the owner has a property super-fluous to their requirements and rather than sell it they decide to rent it.

According to the Australian Bureau of Statistics, 7 per cent of investors rent out a property, often the former family home, after failing to find a buyer for it (ABS 8711.0, Household Investor in Rental Dwellings, Australia).

The same report advises that of the *deliberate* investors in residential real estate 66 per cent purchased an invest-ment property because they wanted a secure long-term investment. Around 20 per cent of the investors under 45 years of age were attracted to the idea of reducing their income tax through negative gearing. Nearly 30 per cent of the older investors, those aged over 65, were looking to provide themselves with an income in the form of rental returns. Of the youngest group of investors, those under the age of 35, 21 per cent purchased an investment property with the eventual aim of living in it themselves.

Many potential investors are uncomfortable with the idea of investing in the share market because of its volatility and the risk of sustaining a loss. They are attracted by the steady growth and seemingly safe option of residential real estate. Many are similar to myself and like to have control over their investments. By choosing property they can have a direct impact on how well that investment performs.

By spending a little to add value to a property, perhaps by repainting walls in modern colours or replacing worn carpets, they can increase the value of their investment far in excess of their outlay. By choosing a property with care and then looking after it, they can maximise their chances of that property increasing in value year after year and ensure that they always have a pool of quality tenants lining up to rent it.

Historically, property values on average rise significantly over any seven- to ten-year period, often doubling their original purchase price. That is to say, if you purchase a property this year, the chances are that in seven years time it will have risen in value, and that per centage increase is often significant. The capital growth may be in the form of a steady increase of 3 or 4 per cent a year, or the value may stagnate for two or three years and then suddenly surge ahead at 20 per cent in one year, as has happened in many areas since the late 1990s all over Australia.

Property values may go down too, but this is rarer, and

over time any slump in the market should even itself out with a corresponding rise. Holding on to your investment property for at least 10 years should see you enjoy a tidy return on your initial investment; choosing this property wisely will almost guarantee that return.

A survey by the Australian Bureau of Statistics showed that of all Australian residential property investors 78 per cent had only one rental property, a further 13 per cent owned two and only 4 per cent owned five or more (Australian Social Trends, 1995, Housing — Housing Stock: Investment in Residential Rental Property). From these figures it would seem highly likely that you would be one of the 78 per cent who buys just one investment property. Therefore it is most important that you choose the right property.

By carefully selecting your investment property, you will hopefully find the whole process so comfortable that you will soon find yourself one of the small per centage of investors with multiple property holdings.

Profile of a tenant

Owning your own home used to be the great Australian dream, but times have changed and many people now prefer to rent. They may well be able to afford a home of their own but they enjoy the flexibility that renting offers them. They can move house whenever they like and not have to worry about the costs of selling and buying another home. Their financial responsibility for their home extends only to paying their weekly rental and the usual utility bills. They do not want to have to concern themselves with maintenance, rates and water bills, building insurance, emergency services levies and all the other myriad taxes successive governments have imposed upon homeowners.

What was that? Neither do you! Well, the good thing about all these fees and charges is that, for the investor, they are all tax deductible.

Of the almost two million Australian households who rent their homes, approximately 74 per cent rent from private landlords, 20 per cent from a state or territory housing authority, and 6 per cent from caravan parks, their employer, a church group or other type of landlord (ABS 1301.01, Survey of Income and Housing Costs, 1999–2000).

In the private rental sector, around 23 per cent of tenants are family units (mums and dads with one or more children). Single parents make up a further 14 per cent and couples 16 per cent. Singles account for 28 per cent (ABS 1301.01). No data is available to show the family unit type and size of the remaining 19 per cent.

These figures are based on an average taken across Australia and the figures may be slightly different according to the area in which your investment property is situated.

At first glance you might be forgiven for thinking that the highest proportion of private tenants is made up of singles. However, if you add together the couples with children and the single parents, these family groups add up to a huge 37 per cent, or around one-third, of all renters.

Some tenants only want to rent in the short term. Since the introduction of the First Home Buyers Incentive, many Australians have had a new home built for them. Others have sold their existing family home to finance a new building venture. Most of them have had to rent a home while their new house was being built. With average local

Council approval times prior to commencement of building being around three months, and the building process itself taking a further four to nine months, these people are often looking for rental accommodation for up to a year.

Other tenants are long term. In this day and age many people cannot obtain a contract of permanent employment and have to rely on permanent casual employment or part-time or seasonal work. Banks and other lending institutions traditionally do not like to lend to people who do not have a stable work history and a permanent full-time job. Unable to obtain a mortgage, even though they may be perfectly financially stable, these people are forced onto the rental market, sometimes for a long time.

Some tenants come from the public housing sector. Stocks of local authority housing have been steadily declining over the past few years, so in an effort to reduce escalating maintenance costs on their increasingly ageing housing stock, authorities have been selling homes to existing tenants. In many cases they have not replaced them with new dwellings. A study in 1997 by the Commonwealth Department of Family and Community Services (Annual Report 1996–97) showed that in the majority of states and territories around half of all applicants for public housing face a waiting list of up to three years.

As a consequence, where a tenant is in receipt of Centrelink social security benefits, the trend is for Centrelink to subsidise the rental on homes rented from private landlords, by providing rent assistance rather than public housing. The state housing authority may even put up the bond in certain circumstances. Sometimes this is in the form of a grant, in other cases it may be in the form of a temporary interest-free loan.

Young singles who are just entering the workforce may also choose to rent accommodation. They may find it hard to save for a deposit on a home of their own because they are more likely to have lower paid jobs, making it difficult to accrue the funds required by a lending organisation to grant them a mortgage. Or they may not want to spend their hard-earned dollars on dull things like mortgages and their associated costs when they can rent a reasonable house for a small weekly outlay by sharing with friends. They are then free to indulge their disposable income on clothes, music and clubbing. (I was twenty-something not so long ago, and I rented for these very reasons.) Or they may conclude that there is plenty of time when they are older to tie themselves to a mortgage and are more than happy to rent in the meantime.

As you can see, there are many reasons why people invest in property and just as many reasons why people choose or need to rent. The bottom line is that there is a large pool of people requiring accommodation, which is good news if you are considering investing in residential property. By choosing an investment property carefully, and maintaining it well, you will be the winner!

Chapter 2

HOW I GOT STARTED

I am sure you will agree that with every plan or goal the hardest part is getting started. Fear of the unknown has stopped many a would-be investor in their tracks. Some people never gather enough courage to make that first step, becoming paralysed by the thought of going into debt. You may or may not be as broke as I was when I began buying real estate, but I bet you one thing — you are as nervous now as I was then. You don't need to be nervous. Plan carefully and you will be successful, whatever your goal.

This is my story. I hope it will give you courage to take that first step.

My path to financial freedom began accidentally. I started off simply by choosing not to rent but to buy my first home. My reason for doing so was not part of a huge investment plan but because buying a home was what we did in those days (and I am only talking 20 years ago). My husband shared my views and together we located a small but pleasant house in the first-time home-buyer bracket and took out what seemed like a massive mortgage to pay for it.

Every penny of my small salary went into paying our mortgage, while my husband had to pay for absolutely everything else — food, clothing, furniture, fuel. I remember one week eating nothing but stewed apples 'liberated' from our neighbours' tree. We simply could not afford to buy food that week.

Our first double bed was donated to us by a neighbour. The bedsprings were broken and during the night they would push up through the mattress, scratching our backs and legs. We took to sleeping with a pair of wire-cutters next to the bed. Whenever a rogue spring would make an appearance we would pick up the wire-cutters and cut it off. After a couple of weeks we had disposed of all the dodgy springs. We actually managed to put off the purchase of a new mattress for over a year.

I think you will agree that we really struggled financially. Over time, however, our salaries slowly increased and the financial situation eased. One of the first things we did was purchase a new bed!

After seven years we decided to move from our native England to Australia. We had to wait for nearly a year for our emigration application to be assessed, and to our joy we were accepted. It may seem like a cliché, but at this time we received our first lesson in the magic of real estate.

In seven years our house had tripled in value — we were at the tail end of a real estate boom. With the money realised from the sale of our house, we could meet the substantial costs associated with emigrating to another country *and* put down a sizable deposit on building a project home in Australia.

When we moved into our new home, we had no carpets, no garden, no heating or cooling, and newspapers on the windows instead of curtains. For the next seven years (our lives seem to revolve around that number!) we spent all our spare cash on establishing the house and garden and buying furniture, cars and holiday trips back to England to visit our parents. We didn't save a cent.

As well as holding down full-time employment, we both took on study to enhance our job skills. Our new skills, together with the intrinsic effect of inflation, gradually led to an increase in our salaries, and soon we had paid off our mortgage. All this added up to an increase in our disposable income and we wanted to spend it wisely.

We decided to purchase an investment property.

My first investment property

It was because we had extra cash in our pockets through no longer having a mortgage to pay that we decided to invest, even though we had no idea what to buy or where to get finance. It is said that with hindsight everyone has 20/20 vision and, looking back, we could easily have afforded the first step towards our investment portfolio much earlier by borrowing against the equity in our home. The important thing was, however, that we had actually made the decision to buy.

We called a local real estate agency that was always running advertisements for 'Real Estate Investment Advice' and made an appointment to see their investment adviser. A few days later we were sitting in his office, feeling nervous and virginal, never having invested in property before. (We never considered that in buying our own home we had made an investment. We thought of that as a lifestyle choice. Of course, now we can see that it was the investment in our own home that allowed us to set out on the path we have subsequently taken.)

The investment adviser shook our hands and whisked

us into his office where he had an impressive looking computer program blinking at us from the monitor on his desk. After we had given this total stranger details of our income and outgoings, he fed the figures into the computer, and a few moments later the printer churned out a page full of charts and numbers.

We were delighted to find that we could easily afford an investment property, in fact we could have more than one if we so desired.

We digested the information we had been given, and talked it over. We were both nervous at the thought of taking out a sizable mortgage to buy an investment property. We asked ourselves why we were thinking of taking this risk. Should we walk away now, forget the investment and spend our extra income on new clothes, holidays and eating out? Life is short after all.

After a few sleepless nights and seemingly endless discussions, we decided to go ahead with the investment idea. The whole purpose of buying the property was to give us financial freedom in our retirement, which was still some 20 years down the track. We both had superannuation, but only the industry minimum, and neither of us wanted to go into retirement on little more than a subsistence wage. At that point we were only considering investing in one property.

We called the agent and asked him if he had any suitable properties on his books. Naturally he had just the very thing.

The very thing turned out to be a five-bedroom, two-storeyed monstrosity in an extremely average suburb, built in the 1970s and extensively added to over the years. The wallpaper, light fittings and carpets were all mismatched and hideous, and the house itself was a rabbit warren of rooms with temporary dividing walls erected to make even more rooms. It was up for sale for $90 000.

We didn't know a thing about property investing, but we certainly didn't like the look of this place. The agent tried his best to sell it to us, explaining that there was hardly any rental accommodation available for families with large numbers of children, and that if we bought the house we would never be without a tenant as we would have something that no-one else could offer.

I don't know about you, but I don't know anyone who has more than three children. I'm sure there are large families out there somewhere, but it seems to me that in the age of the nuclear family they are a minority. We thought we would be restricting our rental market if we took the agent's advice and purchased this property. We could not imagine who would want to rent a huge old place with more rooms than they could ever use. Neither did we want to rent to a family with lots of small children who might wreck the place even more. Kids will be kids after all.

We resisted the agent's appeals to consider the house and a few days later he called us to tell us about another hot property he had on his books. This time it was a small, very neat 1960s home, in the same poor suburb. The street was lined with similar properties on one side, and a train line ran parallel to the street on the opposite side of the road. This time the house was only $76 000 and he was sure we could get $120 rent a week. This would have given us a good return of just over 8 per cent. We couldn't do it. We knew we would never in a million years have wanted to live in that house — it was in such a dismal location — and we figured that if we felt like that prospective tenants would too. We didn't doubt that we could rent it; we just believed that the majority of tenants would turn their noses up at it.

By this time we had started looking in the windows of other real estate agents. We had resisted this at first as we felt some kind of obligation to the first agent — he had put a lot of time into trying to help us. As it happened, his agency had a very attractive little courtyard house advertised in the window. It was only five years old, it was in an up-and-coming suburb, and it was close to shops, schools and transport. We wondered why our agent had not mentioned it to us, and asked him if we could view it.

He started out by telling us that we could see it 'if we wanted to'. It was not a good rental proposition in his opinion. We could buy something far less expensive — the asking price was $92 000 — and get a better rental return on our money. He told us that the house was very well maintained, with neat and attractive gardens planted with a small lawn front and back, some standard roses and a few shrubs. We should bear in mind, he said, that if we rented it out it would never look as good again as it did now. We said we still wanted to see the property and made an appointment for two days time. We then called a finance broker and organised to borrow the necessary finance.

When we viewed the home, it was love at first sight. But better and much more important than the emotions it evoked in us, it had ideal investment potential. The house was attractively proportioned, with three bedrooms, wardrobe space, walk-through access from the main bedroom to the modern three-way bathroom and a spacious open-plan living area. It was painted throughout in a pleasant neutral cream and had plain, serviceable carpets.

It also had a modern air-conditioner and a gas fire and stove. The gardens were neat and low maintenance. The other houses in the street were equally neat and attractive. It was close to the local shops and a number of schools.

We had checked in the local newspaper prior to viewing the house and knew that rents in the area were around $150 per week for similar properties. We offered $90 000 for the house and it was accepted. We later rented it for $155 per week, which gave us a rental return nearly 1 per cent higher than we would have received had we purchased the little house by the railway track. (In the five years since we purchased the house its value has increased by 80 per cent.)

Once we had signed the contract to purchase the property, we decided to engage a property manager. We knew that the agent who had sold us the house had over 800 rental properties registered with his agency. Far from making us feel confident that we would be in experienced hands, this made us feel that ours would be just one of the huge number of properties they had listed and that when we were looking for a new tenant we would be competing with lots of others. We decided to interview a property manager who worked for a small boutique agency in the area in which the house was situated. They would have a much smaller number of properties on their books and our investment was likely to receive more individual attention. This proved to be a good strategy. We will never know if the original agent would have done a good job, but we do know that we were happy with the agent we selected.

An interesting thing happened when we met our soon-to-be property manager for the first time. We were talking about property investment in general, relating our adventures with the first agent and telling her about the properties he had tried to sell us. This is when we found out about all the tax deductions that are available to investors. Incredibly, we had no idea about construction cost write-offs, depreciation and all the other tax concessions open to us. On carrying out some quick calculations we realised that we were better off financially by purchasing the newer, more expensive property. Life can be very kind sometimes.

As I said at the beginning of this chapter, we decided to purchase an investment property so that we could make good use of some of our increased disposable income. Within weeks we realised that paying off the investment property was hardly making a dent in our income. Within six months we had borrowed to purchase a second property. Two years later we bought our third and fourth. Within three years of purchasing our first property the real estate market began to boom, and our properties increased in value. We bought some more. We are still buying, still investing in our future. You can do the same.

My current options

In choosing to invest in residential property I have opened up a world of opportunity for myself. Let's look at my options. *Remember, these could be your options too.*

- I can continue to work at my normal employment and not purchase any additional properties. By doing nothing more than letting the tenant and the taxman pay off my mortgages in less than 20 years I will own all my properties outright. I can then retire at the normal retirement age and enjoy a rental income which will be in excess of my present salary, even allowing for future pay increases and inflation.

- I can continue to stay in my usual employment, but continue buying property. I can expand my portfolio by using the equity built up in each new acquisition to finance the purchase of another investment property. I am not planning to retire soon so all the rental income can go to servicing my ever-increasing mortgage debt. By taking on a larger debt now, while I am still relatively young, I will ensure even greater security in my old age.

- I can retire early. This would mean waiting for seven years or so until the natural cycle of the property market roughly doubles the value of my investments, then selling some of my properties, timing any sales to minimise Capital Gains Tax and using the money to pay off the mortgages on the rest. I could then retire from the workforce early, with enough weekly rental income to live comfortably for the rest of my days — and that income would increase with inflation, unlike many other forms of savings.

- I can wait until my properties have increased in value, and then draw off a loan from the increased equity. I can then bank the loan monies and retire early, perhaps in only a year or two, drawing a small but comfortable income from my bank account. In a few more years my properties should have risen in value again, and I can draw down another equity loan. The rental income will have gone up too, and should pay all, or most, of the loan repayments. This idea is not new but is very often overlooked by property investors — check out www.theinvestorsclub.com.au for details

of many investors who have based their whole investment strategy on this premise.

I have mentioned the above options not to brag about my
own good fortune, but to help you to see that by making a
wise investment decision now, you too could be in a similar
position to me in just a few years. The following chapters
will tell you how to make it happen for *you* and *your*
family.

Chapter 3

HOW YOU CAN GET STARTED

Maybe you already have a home you are paying off, or maybe you're renting but thinking of buying. Whatever your situation, you will need some savings behind you in order to get started on your investment strategy, either in the form of equity that you have built up in your own home or in the form of savings in the bank.

For investment property purchases many institutions will lend the full purchase price plus the associated purchasing costs. In return they will expect you to provide at least 20 per cent of the total costs in the form of a second mortgage over your existing home. If you are serious about investing and do not have equity in an existing home, or cash savings, you may wish to consider raising the deposit by selling or trading down your car or some other asset. For a couple of years you may be consigned to travelling on public transport, but you can ride along bathed in the comfortable knowledge that every day your investment is growing.

Some investors continue to rent homes themselves, as they cannot afford to buy a property to live in but want to get onto the investment ladder. By taking out an investment loan and renting out their property, while continuing to rent or share accommodation, or to live at home with their family, they can enjoy the benefits of the tax breaks legally available to investors. Later on, when their income increases, they can move into their own investment property. Or they may use the equity they have built up in it to raise a deposit for their own home.

Lesser tax breaks are afforded by purchasing a property for investment purposes, living in it yourself and renting out a room or rooms. You can claim only a proportion of the tax concessions and depreciation benefits available, as you are living in the home yourself, but the income you receive from your tenants could mean the difference between being able to purchase the property or not.

Don't even think about looking at prospective investment properties until you have received approval for finance from your chosen lending institution. For the purposes of the next section I will assume that you have prearranged your finances. We will cover lending institutions, mortgages and other necessary evils later in the book.

Choosing the right property

The first thing you need to do is decide on the type of property that will fit within your comfort zone.

This book is aimed at the residential property investor, as the residential rental market is more stable and the returns, although generally lower than commercial property investment yields, are more consistent. Commercial property can offer higher rental returns, but is much more risky. While you may be lucky and find a stable, long-term tenant for your commercial property, do you really want your financial future linked to the fortunes of someone else's business? Businesses come and go, and if your tenant's business does not make it, you could find yourself with an empty building for months, maybe even years, while you wait for another suitable business tenant to come along.

Let's assume that you have decided to make your investment in the residential sector. You now have the choice of units, houses, townhouses, city terraces or cottages — in fact any dwelling someone might like to make their home.

Being comfortable with your borrowing level is an important factor in deciding which type of property you should select for your investment. Your borrowing capacity may be only sufficient to purchase a small outer-suburban unit. As long as it is in an area with plenty of local employment, a transport route and is well located in terms of shops and other amenities, this could be an excellent choice.

If you choose a unit, remember that, in addition to the purchasing costs, you must pay ongoing strata title fees, as most unit blocks employ the services of a strata manager. You will also need to attend regular strata meetings where all interested parties discuss the state of the units in general and decide on such issues as whether to repaint the exterior, replace guttering, and so on. The majority vote decides, so you may find yourself paying to repaint the exterior of your property when you do not believe it needs it. Conversely, you may be outvoted when you want the property repainted and the other parties at the meeting do not. This could result in your property depreciating in value due to the failure of others to agree to general maintenance of the block. These examples are both extreme, but you should be aware that when purchasing into a unit block (unless of course you own the whole block) you will not be the only person making decisions concerning your property.

Having said that, there are some excellent unit blocks in all cities, and if you choose wisely you may well find yourself enjoying many years of incident free ownership.

The demand for property

You want your property to appeal to as many potential tenants as possible. The Australian Bureau of Statistics (ABS 1301.01, Survey of Income and Housing Costs, 1999–2000, www.abs.gov.au) reports that of all renter households 53 per cent live in detached houses and 21 per cent live in townhouses or terraces. A further 26 per cent live in units, flats or apartments. These figures clearly indicate that by far the greatest demand by people wanting rental accommodation is for separate houses.

The wish list

When choosing your investment property, you should make up a wish list of desirable features and stick to it as closely as possible. The items on the list will differ, according to whether you wish to purchase a unit, townhouse or apartment, or whether, like me, you choose to invest in suburban three-bedroom houses. The property you choose may not have everything on the list, but if you take your time and look for long enough you should find one that comes pretty close.

The aim of the wish list is to help you choose a property that appeals to as many potential tenants as possible, and still gives you a reasonable capital gain. You need to make people want your property, so that even when times are tough and the rental market is quiet, you can still pick and choose from the best applicants and command the best possible rent for the area because your property is still in demand.

Wish list for a suburban house

- modern property, attractive from the street
- well cared for (you want to be able to move someone in straightaway)
- 13 squares or more
- fairly quiet street, surrounded by similar quality houses
- within reasonable distance — say, 10 minutes walk — of shops, schools and public transport (bus or train route)
- three bedrooms
- ensuite or walk-through bathroom from main bedroom
- built-in wardrobes in every bedroom
- neutral colours
- vertical blinds in every room (they don't go out of fashion like patterned curtains)
- plain, serviceable carpets without stains (no bold patterns)
- adequate heating and cooling
- carport, preferably under the main roof
- concrete or paved driveway
- garden shed
- medium-sized, easy-care garden, with a few shrubs

Some investors claim that any residential property can be rented because there is never enough to go around. They swear that the size, condition and location of the property are not important. It is my strong belief that if you want to be able to pick and choose from the very

Wish list for a unit or townhouse

- well-maintained block
- within 10 kilometres of the inner city or most popular beaches
- close to shops
- close to public transport
- if possible, within walking distance of cafes, cinemas, entertainment venues, or other such drawcards for young single people
- one or more designated parking bays per unit
- two bedrooms
- built-in wardrobes
- decorated in neutral colours
- plenty of storage space

best available tenants it is wise to choose a property that matches as closely as possible the requirements of the rental sector in which you are interested in investing.

What to avoid

Don't concentrate solely on the attributes of the property. It is pointless buying a great property if all the other houses in the street are neglected and run-down. One daggy house in an otherwise attractive street is not a problem — it could sell tomorrow and be spruced up by the new owners — but a whole street of overgrown gardens and peeling paintwork is bad news. Likewise, if the next-door neighbour has a front garden full of rusting car wrecks. Not many house-proud tenants will want to rent a house next door to a place like that!

There are other less obvious factors you should take into consideration. Is the neighbourhood close to an industrial area from which nasty smells may carry to the property you are thinking of buying? If this occurred regularly, you might find yourself with a high tenant turnover.

A couple of our properties are on an attractive new estate adjacent to what was an old mushroom farm. Back in the days when the mushroom farm was fully operational, the smell of composting mushrooms would waft over the neighbouring houses, sliding insidiously under doors and through air-conditioning vents, making life extremely unpleasant for the residents.

It was not the fault of the owner of the mushroom farm — his farm had been there for years before developers bought up the surrounding land and developed it. Eventually the poor man was forced to relocate because of all the complaints from his new neighbours.

Maybe the property you are looking at is near a school. Check out the street it is in at different times of the day. Does it fill up with the cars of mums doing the school run? This is not necessarily a problem, but it might put off some tenants. Is there a cemetery on the other side of that high back fence? How about a service station or shops? Maybe there is a child-care centre next door? Your tenant wants to be close to amenities, but not necessarily right on top of them and all the associated noise they may generate.

Are all these checks really necessary?
When we first came to Australia, we looked at a few established properties. One was in a semi-rural area which had a huge expanse of vacant land in front of it. The land had

a notice erected on it. We walked over and read the sign. It said: 'Future Site of New Expressway'.

We asked the real estate agent when the expressway was scheduled to be built. He was dismissive. It had been on the cards for years, he told us. It would never go ahead.

We liked the house and were considering buying it. We phoned the local council and asked to speak to the planning department. We asked the man on the other end of the telephone about the plans for the expressway. He replied that the agent was correct, that the expressway had been talked about for years. It was unlikely to go ahead in the near future, but it would go ahead, even if it were not for another 10 years. We decided against buying the house.

Ten years later the new expressway opened. Thousands of cars roar by every day, 20 metres from the front door of the house we were thinking of buying.

Our first house in England was a semi-detached, two-storeyed, 1950s brick home in a wide, tree-lined street. It was opposite a church, and at one end of the street was a pretty little pub. Sounds quite picturesque, doesn't it?

The first Saturday night after we had moved in we were disturbed by the sounds of fighting and swearing in the street outside. It was coming from two drunks walking home from the pub. We hoped it was not going to be a regular occurrence. The next morning, we had been looking forward to lying in and reading the Sunday papers. At 7 am we were woken by the sound of the church bells chiming.

Eventually we became so used to the sound of the bells that we would sleep through them, not even hearing them during bell-ringing practice on Thursday evenings. There was still the occasional loud drunk shouting or singing his way home from the pub at night, but again we learned to shut out the noise. You can get used to anything in time. Your tenants don't have to. They can always move out.

Sometimes you will do all your homework and still hit on a problem. Our second rental property was an extremely nice, spacious modern home in a desirable area. We could not understand why we were experiencing a high turnover of tenants. We had two lots of tenants through in the first year, both breaking their leases with good excuses for leaving. One was a family who wanted to return to Queensland because they missed their relatives; the other was a couple who had decided to purchase their own property. We just assumed that we had been unlucky in our choice of tenants.

It was not until the third tenant moved in and we spent a weekend at the property erecting a pergola for her that we found out why they had *really* both left. The next-door neighbours fought constantly day and night. The language they used had to be heard to be believed, and the decibel level was nearly on a par with a jet fighter passing overhead. They were relentless. Our new tenant shrugged her shoulders and said she would try and stick it out. A few weeks later the neighbours moved out. Crisis over!

The purpose of mentioning all these scenarios is to emphasise that you can only make a choice based on the information available to you. However, the more checks you make, the less likely you are to make the wrong choice. So, if you have checked out every aspect of the area in which you have decided to buy, go out and start looking at properties.

Chapter 4

TYPES OF PROPERTY

Choosing the castle

The purpose of this book is to help you make a secure investment. As you have read in earlier chapters, statistics show that the safest type of residential property to buy is the family home because of the great demand for this type of accommodation. I truly believe that this is your safest option. However, capital growth is likely to be slow and steady rather than a fast track to wealth creation.

A most important factor in choosing an investment property is motivation. You need to be happy with your choice of property. You therefore need to be motivated to research your purchase thoroughly. If the thought of buying a three-bedroom house in suburbia sends you to sleep, and if you're happy to trade off a little of your inner comfort for living on the edge, you may wish to consider a townhouse or beachside unit. Or you may relish the thought of tackling a renovation in the hope of enjoying a large capital gain with which to fund further investments.

So if, after careful appraisal of your local rental market, you have decided to stray from my recommendation of safety in suburbia, you could consider the following types of residential investment property.

Property renovation for capital gain

Investors who can afford to bankroll a renovation program sometimes purchase a run-down or tired property in a good capital growth area. If you take this option, be careful to choose a property in a favourable location within reasonable proximity of all services, such as employment, shops, transport and schools. Cost the renovation before you put in your offer and resist the temptation to renovate outside the style of the original home. Renovation may be as simple as repainting, recarpeting and tidying up the garden, or as extensive as putting in an extra bedroom, replacing an old kitchen and completely refurbishing a bathroom. Costs will vary enormously, depending upon the scope of the renovation and whether you do the work yourself or hire professionals to do it for you. Don't forget that you are unlikely to be able to rent out the property while you are carrying out the alterations, so you will be meeting the cost of the mortgage from your own funds.

However, if you have the stamina and expertise to renovate, this can be a quick path to wealth. Say, for instance, you were to purchase a run-down property in an outer Melbourne suburb for $350 000 and factor in a renovation cost of $40 000. Allowing six weeks from settlement for the renovation to take place, working on it full time or hiring professionals, you then have the place revalued. It is now worth $480 000. You can use the increased equity in this property to raise a mortgage for a further investment property. Conversely, you may decide to sell it for a quick financial gain (remember you will have to pay tax on your profit).

Sounds good, doesn't it? If you decide to go down this path, be aware that you are taking a bigger risk, and make sure that you have planned for every eventuality. Don't carry out improvements to a property that are not going to return a profit — what is to be gained from spending $15 000 on a new kitchen if this improvement is only going to add $15 000 to the total value of the property? (There are some excellent books available on renovating for profit — check with your local bookshop or library.)

Beachside properties

People think that there is some sort of mystery in purchasing beachside property and go to great lengths to try and forecast the next boom area. However, it is not really any different from investing in any other sort of residential property. In recent years Australians have caught on to the appeal of living on the coast and property values in such areas, especially for houses with absolute beachfront positions, have rocketed. It may be that this particular horse has bolted and prices will not rise as spectacularly again. Nevertheless, beachside living will always have appeal.

Well known traditionally for attracting young singles and retirees, beachside living has caught the attention of more and more families in recent years, pushing up the prices of houses along the coast beyond the reach of most first-time property investors. However, if you are attracted by the possibility of higher capital gain and a likely lower rental yield, or are considering purchasing such a property with the eventual aim of living in it yourself, then a seaside location may be just right for you.

Townhouses

One of the great appeals of townhouses for investors is often cited as the low maintenance involved in owning such properties. Often having little or no garden and common walls, all of which cut down on outdoor maintenance responsibilities for you, as landlord, townhouses can be a very good investment. They don't tend to attract family groups as tenants, but rather lend themselves to professional singles and couples, and shared households. For many investors, these are the ideal tenants as they are less likely to have children or pets and more likely to be out at work all day, putting less stress on the home in terms of wear and tear. However, I still believe that suburban family homes will offer you a higher pool of tenants to choose from and a greater number of buyers should you decide for any reason that renting is not for you and wish to sell. Townhouses are quite often strata title or community title, so be sure to read up on your rights and obligations under the relevant Acts.

Units

Units can be a very attractive option for the residential investor. They often carry higher depreciation opportunities than other forms of property, as they have a smaller land component and the majority of the purchase price relates to the actual building.

One drawback is that your tenant will be living in close proximity to others. Unless you own the whole complex, you will have no control over who lives in the other units. This is of course true for all property: you cannot control who your neighbours will be. But for units this can be a very important issue. If you have chosen a nice, quiet young couple, or a genteel retired lady, as your tenant, and the people in the next-door unit — with walls common to yours — are noisy partygoers, you will either find yourself embroiled in disputes or wondering why your tenants keep quitting on you.

On the other hand, if your unit complex has appealing common areas and amenities such as a shared swimming pool or communal garden — and a good strata management team in place — it is likely that your tenants will enjoy living in your unit, as they will be free from worry about its upkeep.

High-rise apartments

As I write this, there is an explosion of high-rise apartments in Perth, Adelaide, Melbourne, Sydney, Brisbane and the Gold Coast. The general consensus of opinion among property experts is that the rate of construction will eventually lead to an oversupply of such dwellings, with a possible downturn in property values and an increase in vacancy rates. If you wish to purchase an inner-city apartment with the future aim of moving into it yourself, this would be a reasonable decision; as purely an investment, however, I would not recommend it over other types of property.

The insurance regulations for high-rise apartments, units and townhouses are more complex than for single homes on individual blocks. The cost of building policies for strata blocks is split between the owners of the individual dwellings, and you should check carefully that the amount of insurance cover is adequate. Be aware that strata insurance only covers the common areas of the strata complex, so you may find that air-conditioners, hot water systems and other building related improvements specific to your unit are not covered. Public liability insurance does not extend to cover inside individual dwellings, being similarly restricted only to common areas. You should take out a separate contents insurance policy to cover your personal effects, such as carpets, curtains and so on, just as you would for a single dwelling.

Chapter 5

PROPERTY STATE BY STATE

Following is a broad overview of property in the capital cities and the Gold Coast, which will hopefully prove useful as a starting point to your research, together with information on some of the traps it is easy for the novice investor to fall into. My thanks to Quartile Property Network for the statistics quoted in this chapter. As the latest property data is released three months after the end of each quarter, you might like to visit them at www.quartile.com.au for the latest market data.

Sydney

Unquestionably Australia's most famous city, Sydney is a rambling sprawl set on the shores of the one of the world's most beautiful harbours. Property prices are extremely high compared with those of the less populous states and territories, for example, South Australia, Tasmania and Western Australia.

At the time of writing, anecdotal evidence suggests that it is a tenants' market in Sydney, as there is an oversupply of rental properties. The result is that tenants can pick and choose which property to lease and landlords are forced to reduce rents or offer incentives, such as two weeks rent free, to new tenants in order to attract them.

In December 2002 the vacancy rate in Sydney was

around 4.5 per cent. This means that around 45 of every 1,000 properties available for rental in Sydney were vacant at any one time during that period.

If you have done your homework and thoroughly investigated the area and type of property in which you would like to invest, this need not be a major problem for you. When you are looking at the amount you can afford to borrow and the price and rental return of properties in your chosen area, you should factor in a two-week period every year when the property may be vacant. If you also ensure that you purchase a quality property, you are more likely to be one of the 955 out of 1,000 landlords who rent their properties relatively easily. Do not confuse 'quality' with 'expensive' — you can purchase a small, plain, well cared-for house for the same money as a small, plain, badly looked after one.

In December 2002 median rents in Sydney were $245 per week for a three-bedroom house and $270 per week for a two-bedroom unit. Be aware that these are median rents only, and there will be large variations in these figures depending on the area in which the property is located, the condition of the property and the number of properties of the same type available for rent. For example, there may be a shortage of townhouses, but a glut of units, or vice versa. Take a look at the case studies of investors and tenants in the Appendix and you will see that three-bedroom houses can bring over $400 per week.

For new investors a cautious approach would be advisable in 2003 as experts are tipping the Sydney market to fall (some say by up to 20 per cent). Start watching the market, reading the real estate sections in the newspapers and keeping track of prices. If they seem to be falling, you might decide to wait a while until you purchase, in the hope that prices will fall even further or at least until they appear to have stabilised. Remember, knowledge is power. If you want to minimise the risks of investing in property, make sure you get to know the area in which you intend to buy, so that you can recognise a fair market price when you see one.

Melbourne

A gracious city, home to over three million people, Melbourne has enjoyed some reasonable capital gains over the past 12 months. Towards the end of 2002 the vacancy rate for rental properties rose fairly rapidly from 3.8 per cent in June 2002 to 4.1 per cent in the December quarter. In December 2002 the median purchase price for houses was $335 000 and $268 500 for units. No data was available on weekly rental figures, but in the June quarter the median rent for units was $190 per week, while for a three-bedroom house it was $220 per week.

As with Sydney, it would be wise to exercise some caution before purchasing. Ensure that you do your research and determine the direction of the market before you buy. Waiting a few months may save you thousands of dollars. However, don't forget that when purchasing for the long haul the starting point is not as important as the finishing point. A house bought for $350 000 today might be worth $700 000 in 10 years. It is only if you need to sell before the market starts to rise again that you might find that the fall in prices — especially if you bought with an interest only loan — has left you out of pocket. My own strategy is to buy wisely and never to sell.

Brisbane

Glorious capital of Queensland, Brisbane experienced fairly

stagnant prices for some years before surging ahead over the past year or two. Historically, Brisbane has offered some good rental yields, and vacancy rates are still low at 3.4 per cent. In December 2002, the median purchase price of houses was \$256 000 and of units \$180 000, with median rents at \$200 per week and \$180 per week respectively.

Gold Coast

The beautiful beaches of the Gold Coast are only an hour's drive from Brisbane, and many residents find it relatively easy to commute to the CBD. Potential investors in Gold Coast property should be alert to the many, many glitzy high-rise developments all along the coast which, although very attractive, are well into oversupply. However, other types of residential property, purchased to supply the fast-growing local population could prove to be a very good investment. Anecdotal evidence suggests that vacancy rates for such properties are relatively low, with some growth left in the market.

Other capital cities

All around Australia vacancy rates are 5 per cent or less, with Darwin the highest and Hobart and Adelaide the lowest at approximately 2 per cent. Perth and Canberra are somewhere in between.

No matter where you live, what style of property you wish to invest in, or where you intend to purchase that property, the name of the game is BE INFORMED.

Beware of buying interstate property

There are agents who specialise in selling real estate to buyers in other states. While there is nothing inherently wrong with this, some agents will employ less than fair tactics in a bid to attract unwary interstate buyers. These agents advertise in national newspapers to encourage investors to contact them or to attend 'free' investment property seminars, knowing that at least some investors do not know the areas in which these agents are selling and therefore do not know what the true market value of property is for those areas. The agents send them details of attractive, often brand new units or townhouses, with details of the asking prices and projected rentals.

Some agents even fly investors interstate to view a range of properties — at the agent's expense. Be aware that the cost of the airfare, accommodation and other expenses will probably be added into the purchase price of the property.

The investor likes a property — it is brand new, so what is there not to like? It is near popular beaches and is in an upmarket complex with a swimming pool and other shared amenities. They sign a contract to buy the place without even considering whether the asking price is representative of the area. Often it turns out to be many thousands of dollars above the true price for a similar property and the investor is not able to sell it without making a substantial loss.

If the investor chooses to keep the property and rent it out, its true value will eventually rise and in a few years it may be worth what they paid for it. In the meantime, they have been ripped off and will probably never purchase another investment property. To quote an old chestnut, there is no such thing as a free lunch.

Beware of rental guarantees
From time to time you may see properties advertised with

a rental guarantee. These are often apartments in new complexes, either in a capital city or in popular beachside suburbs.

When the real estate market is enjoying a building boom you will find developers everywhere, all hoping to take advantage of the boom and make some serious money. This can lead to an oversupply of similar properties, all aimed at the same market.

The easiest way for a developer to get a head start over their rivals is by offering their properties with a rental guarantee. This can be anything from 7 to 9 per cent per year. Sometimes it is accompanied by a promise of zero property management fees.

In order to guarantee you this relatively high return, developers need to ensure they have plenty of money in reserve. Therefore, they will put up the asking price of the apartment by a substantial amount, usually twice the annual dollar difference between the average rent for a similar property and the weekly rental amount they are promising you. For the period of the guarantee you will receive the higher rent, which you have already paid for in the purchase price, and the developer will keep any of the money left over from topping up your rental income.

Once the guarantee period is over, it is possible that rents will have risen and you will continue to achieve a similar rent for your property. More likely, however, you will find yourself dropping the rent to attract a tenant.

You now know all about rental guarantees, but you really do want to buy that city apartment. You can always negotiate with the developer. You have nothing to lose by making a low offer and telling the developer to forget the rental guarantee. He might just take it.

Take care when buying new property

The tax benefits of buying a new property can be substantial. The construction cost and depreciation write-off amounts will be high, as the property is brand new and therefore the true cost of the asset can be depreciated. With established properties, it is the value of the asset at the time of purchase that is depreciated (the exception being the construction cost). For depreciation purposes, a carpet that has been in place for five years is going to start off at a different rate than one that has been newly laid.

Newly built properties are usually more expensive to purchase than established ones of a similar size in a similar area. GST is also payable on the purchase price.

If the builder has not provided certain amenities in the purchase price, you will have to supply these. Check whether driveways, concrete floors to carports, air-conditioning, heating, carpets, curtains or blinds, and built-in wardrobes are being supplied or whether you will have to pay for these on top of the price of the house. You may also have to establish the garden and provide a mailbox, garden shed, clothes line and maybe a pergola or paved outdoor entertaining area.

Some builders provide a total package, others don't. You may be able to clinch a deal whereby you ask the builder to throw in a driveway or ducted air-conditioning for no charge and in return pay the current asking price. Just make sure you check exactly what you are going to get for your money, and that it is all clearly written into the Contract of Sale before you sign it.

Lastly, you should also be aware that you are required to make payments in stages to the builder while the property is under construction. During this period you won't receive any rental income and all costs will have to be supported by you, although you will be able to claim a tax deduction on interest paid if you borrowed the money to build.

Case studies of my rental properties

Whenever I talk to other investors I am always interested to hear details about their properties: what rents they are achieving and what is their turnover of tenants, for example. By also exchanging information on areas, types of properties, real estate agents and property management companies, we can help each other. One extremely successful investor I recently met swears by units and townhouses of which he has many. Another invests in executive rentals in a higher price bracket because they can offer a higher capital gain. Drawing on the experiences of others helps us choose the best investments for our own individual circumstances and goals.

For this reason, listed below are the broad details of some of my own properties.

As you already know, I favour suburban family homes in the top end of the first-time buyer bracket. While they all have many of the features on my wish list, they don't have them all. See if you can guess which ones I have experienced problems renting.

1. A three-bedroom brick veneer house in a popular outer suburban area, set on the low side of the road. The house is around 16 squares, with built-in wardrobes in every bedroom, ducted air-conditioning, gas space heating, large family room and walk-through access from the main bedroom to the bathroom. It is tidy but not exceptional, with a fairly average garden. It is opposite an attractive park, but there is a 20-minute walk to the local shops and schools.

2. A modern 12 square courtyard home, with open plan
   kitchen/dining/lounge area, three bedrooms and a
   built-in wardrobe in the main bedroom only. It has a
   wall-style air-conditioner and a gas heater. Outside there
   is a pleasant patio area with a pergola. The home has
   two-street access, with a carport at the front and extra
   parking at the rear. It is five minutes walk from a
   shopping centre, a bus route and primary schools.
3. A 15 square brick veneer home in a pleasant housing
   estate, a half-hour drive from the city centre. It has
   three bedrooms, all with built-in wardrobes. The main
   bedroom has an en suite. There is a separate lounge
   room, and a combined kitchen and family room. The
   property is on a fairly large block, situated on a quiet
   corner. The garden is quite extensive, with large lawn
   areas. In the backyard is a double garage, and there is
   a carport under the main roof. It is within five minutes
   of schools, shops and public transport.
4. An 11 square home in a popular street of a newer
   residential area. The front door opens straight into the
   lounge room, and it has a combined kitchen and
   family area. It does not have an en suite or
   walk-through access to the bathroom. It has three
   bedrooms, with a built-in wardrobe in the main
   bedroom only. The house has a particularly attractive
   frontage with lots of street appeal. The gardens are
   neat and tidy, with fairly large lawns and lots of
   easy-care shrubs. The driveway of the property is
   white gravel. It has a carport under the main roof.

So tell me, which of them do you think I have problems
renting?

In fact, none of them has ever been vacant.

Number 2 and number 4 have been rejected by some prospective tenants as being a little small, but these have been balanced out by the number of single people, couples and smaller families who have lined up to take them. Both properties are in excellent locations and have lots of street appeal.

Number 1 is a large home with all the creature comforts, which has rented consistently. All the tenants have had their own cars and presumably have driven to the shops and schools. Number 3 has proved extremely popular with gardening enthusiasts, and in fact the garden looks better now than when we first bought the property, thanks to their loving ministrations. Currently, it has a long-term tenant who hopes to stay for many years to come. In fact, all four properties are rented to long-term tenants, a couple of whom have been living there for three years or more.

My properties have all been bought on the basis that if we would be happy to live there others would too. We have a strict rule that if either my husband or myself does not like a property, for any reason, we do not buy it — even if the other thinks it is a good investment prospect. There will always be another property to purchase, one that you both agree on — and who wants to take the risk of having their partner saying 'I told you so' some years down the track if the property turns out to be a dud? Of course, if you are buying on your own, you will have the luxury of buying anything you like! If it turns out to be a good investment, you can congratulate yourself; if it turns out to be a rotten deal, you can quietly sell it.

Chapter 6

WHAT TO LOOK FOR AND
WHAT TO AVOID

As mentioned in previous chapters, I believe that a well-chosen property in the top per centile of the first-time home-buyer bracket represents the minimum risk for investors. There are more long-term tenants renting in this bracket than in any other, and if you decide that investing in property is not for you, there should be a greater market for the property as it will fall within the first-time buyer and home-investor category.

The family home
If you have decided to follow my recommendation, location is important. Our properties are all on attractive housing developments in the outer suburbs of our capital city and all were built after 1985. Such properties seem to appeal to families, who are our target tenants.

Today's families tend to be smaller than those of the 1950s, many including only one or two children. Even so, the hassle of moving every year to a new rental property seems to be greater for families than for single people — they generally have a lot more possessions, making it more difficult and more costly to move. In addition, the children usually go to local schools and have built up a network of friends in the area. Once families find somewhere they like, they tend to stay, often becoming long-term renters.

Selecting a property within a 20–25 kilometre radius of the CBD brings with it a price range that balances well with the rental achieved. Of course, Melbourne and Sydney investors may find they need to purchase further out, while buyers in large regional centres may be able to purchase closer to the centre.

Generally speaking, houses closer to the city centre cost more. Although weekly rents are higher than for an outer suburban property, the actual yield (the rent expressed as a per centage of the purchase price) is usually lower. If you are planning to sell your investment property after a few years, houses close to the city will usually realise a higher capital gain than those in the suburbs. The trade-off is the lower rental yield.

Avoid properties in run-down areas, whether in the inner city or in the suburbs. Don't ignore a property's poor surroundings and condition and purchase it just because it is cheap. You will quite likely find someone to rent it, but in my opinion you will be taking an unnecessary risk. Such homes attract problem tenants, those that other landlords have rejected, often with good reason.

Older homes in the outer suburbs may have a fairly low purchase price, when compared with inner-suburban, city and newer homes, but owing to their age will often require more in the way of maintenance. The cost of repairs and replacement fittings will all come out of your pocket, which in the early years of investment is something you wish to avoid.

A new home, or at least one under 10 years old, is likely to have fewer maintenance problems than an older property.

The trade-off may be that you will have to pay a little more for the newer house, but the extra outlay is generally worth it in terms of a relatively hassle-free existence as a landlord. In addition, the depreciation on a newer home is usually more than for an older property, which will be beneficial for you in terms of taxation deductions.

Your dream home
If you are looking for an up-market investment property, perhaps with the intention of moving into it yourself at a later stage, you may have to trade off some of the 'must haves' of potential tenants in order to purchase the property of your dreams. By doing this, you will be increasing your risk factor slightly, but you may feel that it is worth it. Typical of such properties are expensive beachfront apartments and large homes in trendy inner-city areas, which may rent for very high returns but have a smaller tenant market from which to select. These properties need not necessarily be close to public transport, as the tenants who rent them will usually have one or more cars and no need for buses or trains. Similarly, the tenant is likely to drive to the supermarket so proximity to shops is not an issue.

Units and townhouses
Make sure you choose a reasonably roomy unit with no shared walls. It should not be hard to find a group of units where the only wall shared is with a carport or garage. The last thing a tenant wants is to share their home with their next-door neighbour's music — or — even worse, the flushing of their toilet!

If you decide to purchase a townhouse, make sure that it has at least one designated car space (preferably under cover), a private garden of some description and plenty of natural light in the downstairs areas. Too many townhouses I have inspected are dark and gloomy on the ground floor.

When selecting a unit or townhouse, choose a location within 10 kilometres of the city. In my experience young people and young couples tend to rent units, townhouses and flats which are close to their city or regional centre, or to popular beaches. They like to be reasonably near, or at least on a direct public transport route, to nightlife, cafe strips, cinemas and other entertainment venues, as well as to local employment hubs, such as business districts or industrial estates. They also prefer to be close to local shops.

Which suburb?

Once you have a rough idea of where you want to buy, ring a few real estate agents in that area and ask to speak to their property manager. Ask them which suburbs, in their opinion, have the highest demand for rental properties. Compare the answers the various managers give you to see which suburbs are consistently mentioned. You can then make an informed decision on where to concentrate your search for an investment property.

Next, drive around the suburbs where you intend to buy (you'll find yourself doing a lot of driving during this preliminary stage!). Check out the property in the real estate agents' windows. Look on the Internet, and in the newspapers. You will soon get a good idea of what is available and can start inspecting some properties.

When you inspect a property, imagine that you are the potential tenant and take a good look at it. Is it in good condition? Will it be warm in winter and cool in summer? Is it bright and airy or dark and dingy?

Set aside your personal preferences, and ask yourself, 'If I had to live here for a year or more, is there anything I would be really unhappy with?' For example, you might think it perfect, except for the lack of heating. So think about how much it would cost you to put in a reliable heater? If the cost is within your budget, build it into the purchase cost and buy the property.

Investment property don'ts

The following features fall within a category I call 'Investment Property Don'ts'. In short, if you are buying for investment only and not as a future home for yourself, don't buy a property with one or more of the following features.

Swimming pool

A swimming pool may well get you a new tenant in summer as the water looks cool and inviting and they are mentally planning their first pool party. Unless you are happy to organise regular pool maintenance, and have built that cost into the rent, that lovely blue water may well be green and smelly next time you set eyes on it. Repairs to swimming pools and pool equipment such as pumps can be extremely expensive, and the cost of filling a pool with fresh water can be exorbitant. Who will bear it — you or your tenant?

Finally, and far worse that any of the above, is the prospect of a tenant's child or pet drowning in your pool. Better not to have one in my opinion.

Garage pit

Whilst a garage with a pit may appeal to the amateur car mechanic, you can do without the hassle of a tenant falling into it and breaking a leg. Tenants are not necessarily care-less, but accidents do happen, so why invite one?

Spa

Unless you are buying an executive rental property, both indoor and outdoor spas are just another expense waiting to happen. A new pump can run into thousands of dollars, and you are not even getting the enjoyment from it.

Electronic devices

These include a range of things, from gas fires with elec-tronic control panels and electronically operated roller shut-ters and alarm systems to computer controlled watering systems. They are not, strictly speaking, property don'ts — I would not reject a property that had one or all of these electronic features for this reason alone. Just be aware that they can cost a lot of money to fix and that they can, and do, break down. If your tenant has been making use of such a device, you will be expected to pay for it to be repaired.

Timber window frames

Think of all the maintenance awaiting you — timber will eventually rot and need replacing, and at the very least it will need repainting or revarnishing every few years. Timber window frames can look fantastic when new, but I'd recommend an aluminium frame over a timber one any day.

Location and maintenance

The location of your investment property is important not just to the potential tenant in terms of its proximity to shops, transport, employment and entertainment, but also to you, the investor, in terms of maintaining it. As my husband attends to all of our investment property maintenance, our properties are all within short drive of our own home, albeit in fairly new suburbs which promise a reasonable potential for growth.

If you intend to leave absolutely everything to your property manager and employ tradesmen to fix all maintenance problems, only giving a thought to your investment at tax time, then having your property close to your home may not matter to you. Indeed, you are free to seek out and research areas that are being tipped for growth and have good potential for capital gain without worrying about how far away they are for maintenance purposes.

Chapter 7

ARRANGING YOUR FINANCE

Once you have gained a fairly accurate idea of what type of property you wish to buy, in what location and in what price bracket, it is time to work out just how you are going to finance this adventure. As mentioned previously, don't even think about putting in an offer on a property without prearranging your finance.

Contact two or three mortgage brokers — they will come to your home, at your convenience, and will have a selection of mortgages from which to choose. After discussing your personal situation with you, they should be able to offer you a mortgage product from one or more finance houses to suit your individual circumstances. Alternatively, you may already have a good relationship with your bank or credit union, so talk to them about the mortgage facilities they can offer you.

Do not be afraid to negotiate. Tell your prospective lender that you are considering other lending institutions. Ask them to waive the application fee, or perhaps the valuation fee, in order to make the offer more attractive to you, or ask what incentive they are prepared to offer in order to gain your business. Sometimes the lender will come back with an offer far better than you had even hoped for. The worst case scenario would be that they say 'take it or leave it' in which case you have lost nothing and can indeed 'leave it' if that is what suits you.

Make sure that you have your financial details prepared before the meeting. You want to impress on the broker or bank manager that you have thought out your investment strategy and can afford to comfortably repay the moneys you wish to borrow. Take to the meeting:

• payslips for the last two months to illustrate your current earnings
• particulars of any other income, from investments, bank interest, etc.
• details of your non-financial assets, such as your house, car and boat, including their current worth
• details of savings you wish to use as your deposit (this may be in the form of equity in your own home)
• details of loans you have taken out (mortgages, car loans, credit cards)
• estimate of the weekly rental you expect to receive from the property.

The broker will need to know how much you wish to borrow. Don't forget to allow for purchasing costs on top of the purchase price: on a $200 000 property these will be in the order of $10 000. They include stamp duty on the purchase price of the property, which varies from state to state, and can also be borrowed from the bank.

Detailed below are the main purchasing costs, state by state, on the above investment property loan:

	Stamp duty on amount borrowed	Stamp duty on property purchase	Transfer fee	Mortgage registration fee
ACT	$0	$5500.00	$155.00	$ 78.00
NSW	$781.00	$5490.00	$ 60.00	$ 60.00
NT	$0	$6800.00	$ 90.00	$ 90.00
QLD	$840.00	$5600.00	$143.00	$100.00
SA	$725.00	$6830.00	$875.00	$ 90.50
TAS	$725.00	$5675.00	$ 10.00	$ 85.50
VIC	$804.00	$7660.00	$582.00	$ 59.00
WA	$787.50	$6350.00	$105.00	$ 75.00

In Queensland there are differing rates of stamp duty for properties bought as a residence and properties bought as an investment. (The figures above are for an investment property.) As a rough guide, the stamp duty payable on an investment property in Queensland is around three times as much as on a property purchased as a residence.

As with all state and federal taxes and duties, the above rates are liable to change at any time, so you should check with your state government as to the current stamp duty rates when you are calculating the purchasing costs for a new investment.

Additionally, you will have to meet the cost of the registration of transfer (to register the property in your name), which on a property with a purchase price of $200 000 ranges from around $60 in New South Wales to $855 in South Australia. Add mortgage stamp duty on the amount borrowed (payable in all states, but not in the territories), conveyancer's fees, land title searches and reimbursement of water and council rates already prepaid by the vendor, and you will soon have around $4000 to find on top of the stamp duty purchasing costs detailed above.

Most lenders will lend up to 80 per cent of a property's valuation. Note that the valuation they will base their offer on will be provided to them by an independent valuer of their choosing, *not* the real estate agent who has put a value, or selling price, on the property. The valuer will base their valuation on the prices achieved for similar properties in the area that have recently sold and will also take into consideration the state of the market (which may be rising, steady or falling).

If the valuation is less than the agreed selling price, you will be offered finance on 80 per cent of the lower figure. If you cannot cover the shortfall with your own funds, the financial institution may offer you the required loan, but insist that you pay mortgage insurance. This covers them if you cannot meet the repayments and they have to sell the property for less than the amount of the money lent. It does not cover you. In fact, after paying out your lending institution, the insurers will approach you for the shortfall. Mortgage insurance is typically anywhere between 1 and 3 per cent of the insured amount, and can run into several thousand dollars, depending on how much you wish to borrow. If you cannot afford to purchase an investment property without having to pay mortgage insurance, I would suggest that you cannot afford to buy that particular property and should set your sights a little lower.

Banks and other lending institutions have been in this game a lot longer than you, and they know a good risk when they see one. If they don't believe you are capable of paying back a loan, take a good look at your circumstances, and ask yourself if they are right.

If you are using your home as collateral, be aware that some financial institutions will not advise you if the valuation figure falls short of the agreed purchase price. They will lend you the money anyway, provided you have enough equity in your own home to cover the shortfall.

Having said all that, if you firmly believe that with the help of rental income and tax breaks you can afford to comfortably pay back the loan you want even though you have been knocked back by the first lender you have approached, don't take no for an answer. Apply to other lenders.

When I got my first loan I was very naive. The lender offered me a good interest rate of half a per cent under the standard variable rate. This was great for the first and second investment properties. Eighteen months later the rent I was obtaining from the two properties coupled with a pay rise and a shift downward in the interest rates meant that I could comfortably afford to purchase two more investment properties. My bank would not even consider a further loan. They wanted me to wait a year and, what is more, instead of exploring my options with other lenders, I waited! In that year property prices started to skyrocket, so that when I eventually got my loan approval for the next two properties the value of houses in my price bracket had risen by an average of $15 000. Learn from my mistakes. Don't take no for an answer, and check out all the available avenues before making any final decision on finance.

Do not get sentimental when shopping for your investment loan. You owe it to yourself to obtain the best financial deal. Lenders know that they will not get a sale on every presentation they make. Of course they are hoping to win your business, but there is no need to feel that you have wasted their time if, in the end, you decide to take up a mortgage with another lender. You have given your broker an opportunity to sell to you and if you decide, after listening to his offer, that you can get a better deal elsewhere, then take it. It sounds tough, but let's face facts — a friendly broker or financial services manager is going to forget your face the moment your meeting is over. You are a prospect: that is all. Be nice to him and treat him with respect, but do not be misled into thinking he is your best friend.

Once you have decided on the lender to which you are going to give your business, concentrate on building a relationship with them. I have a great relationship with my current lender. They understand exactly what I am trying to achieve and we work well together. In turn, I am happy to pay them a fair interest rate in return for their service. They make money, I make money, we are all happy.

Types of loans

There are many loan options available to borrowers these days, and these are outlined below.

Standard variable principal and interest loan

The most popular type of loan product seems to be the standard variable principal and interest loan — your loan repayments consist of interest and partial repayment of capital. These may be secured over varying lengths of time, with 25 years being fairly representative of the majority of the population. If interest rates rise, your repayments also rise; if interest rates fall, your repayments also fall. You can usually make additional repayments, either as a lump sum or by paying back more than the minimum monthly repayment on a regular basis. These extra payments are taken straight off the principal component of the loan and effectively reduce the amount of interest you need to pay on the amount still outstanding, shaving years off your loan repayment period. Most lenders will also allow you to make fortnightly, rather than monthly, repayments. As there are 26 fortnights in a year and only 12 months, you are actually making an extra payment each year, and your mortgage term will reduce accordingly.

Some lenders offer loans that reduce daily. Effectively, this means that if you make a lump sum payment the principal owing is immediately reduced by the amount paid, and the interest owing is immediately adjusted rather than waiting for a set day in the month. Thus the more often you make payments, the faster you pay off your mortgage and the less interest you pay. If you can secure a loan that offers this desirable feature, you may wish to make your loan repayments weekly instead of fortnightly or monthly.

There is also a very similar loan product on the market, called a basic variable principal and interest loan. This is essentially the same as the standard variable product, but some features, such as being able to convert some of the loan to fixed interest (see split loan below), may not be available to you. It may also attract a monthly fee.

Interest only loan

Not nearly so popular among home-buyers, but increasingly attractive to investors, is the interest only loan. With this type of loan the borrower pays only the interest due and nothing off the principal. The rate can be variable or fixed, and generally the loan is taken over a short period, usually between one and five years. Remember, you are not paying anything off the principal! At the end of the loan period you will still owe the total amount of the original loan. At the end of the fixed period the loan may be paid out (if you have the necessary funds saved) or a new loan may be negotiated with either your existing institution or a new lender.

The danger with this type of loan is that if property prices stagnate (as they do, sometimes for two or three years at a time) and you decide that you wish to sell your property during this period, you will still owe the total purchase price. After accounting for purchasing and selling costs, you may find that you have made a loss.

The advantage of interest only loans is that the repayments are much lower than for a principal and interest loan and therefore you should have more disposable income. If you don't have a mortgage on your own home, this disposable income can be saved and either used for a deposit on a further investment property or for regular extra payments against the loan, thus reducing the interest payable. This in turn reduces the size of the loan and gives you equity in the investment. You can usually redraw this equity if you wish, but in the meantime you are paying less interest.

However, if you are still paying off a mortgage on the home in which you are living, the best strategy is to pay any extra income from your investment property into your own home mortgage. The mortgage on your own home is being met by after-tax income, and you are receiving no tax advantage. It therefore makes sense to pay as much off this loan as possible, and once you have paid off your mortgage, you can start paying off the loan on your investment property.

Fixed rate loan

Fixed rate loans can be either interest only, or principal and interest. The interest rate on the loan is fixed for a pre-determined period, usually one to five years, after which you can renegotiate with the bank based on its current interest rates. Fixed rate loans are designed to protect you against large increases in interest rates. Say you take on a fixed rate of 6.5 per cent and interest rates later rise to 7.25 per cent, you will still be paying 6.5 per cent.

The obvious disadvantage in taking on a fixed rate loan of any description, whether interest only or principal and interest, is that if interest rates fall you will be left paying the higher rate on your loan until the end of the loan agreement. The penalties for refinancing such a loan are often very high. If your mortgage is only relatively small, you may prefer to take the variable rate option. However, for large loans, an interest rate rise of even 1 per cent can add hundreds of dollars to your monthly repayment. For this reason I prefer to fix my loans.

Another disadvantage of fixed rate loans is that often the lender will not allow additional repayments during the fixed term, or limits them to a fairly small amount — for example, no more than an additional $10 000 per annum.

Capped loans

Capped loans are usually offered to new borrowers for the first year of their mortgage. The loan is capped at an agreed rate of interest, say 4.99 per cent for the first year, after which it reverts to the bank's current variable interest rate. If interest rates fall during the first year, you will pay the lower rate on your loan. However, should rates rise, your loan would be capped, or fixed, at the agreed rate of 4.99 per cent.

All-in-one loan

This type of loan is generally linked to a credit card. Your salary is paid directly into your loan account, which is used for your mortgage, your savings and all your day-to-day living expenses. You pay all your monthly outgoings by credit card. At the end of each month, before the expiry of the interest-free period on your credit card, you draw out enough money to pay off the balance owing on your card. All the while your salary is sitting untouched in your bank account, it is reducing the balance of your mortgage loan, and there is a corresponding decrease in the amount of interest being charged. It is also likely that you will leave in the account any moneys left over from your salary, which further reduces the amount of interest owing. The credit card is interest free (except for cash withdrawals or purchases made overseas).

All-in-one loans are a bonus for disciplined people who are able to reduce the term of their home loans by years through using this facility. They never forget to pay off their entire credit card account before the end of the interest-free period, and they never dip into their surplus funds to pay for holidays, cars or other treats. Good luck to those people. However, if you are the sort of person who likes a little splurge and really enjoys the good things in life, then my advice is to avoid all-in-one loans. Without incredible self-discipline, you could soon find yourself deeply in debt.

Line of credit

This type of loan is secured against a mortgage over your property. This may seem obvious, but you can set up a separate line of credit against the equity you have built up in your home. The lender will specify a set credit limit. For a home worth $250 000 for which you still owe $130 000 on your mortgage, the lender may set up a second mortgage with a line of credit of up to $70 000. You are then given a cheque book and can use this money when you need it. Used prudently, this can be very useful if you need cash for the short term, say to put down a deposit on an investment property. You can then pay off the line of credit as soon as the funds for the new purchase come through from the bank. If you use the line of credit to purchase a car or a holiday, you will soon find that you have reduced the equity in your home and are now paying off two mortgages instead of one.

Split loans

These products have been available for a couple of years. They are a combination of variable rate and fixed rate loans, and allow you to hedge your bets. While the variable portion of the loan may rise, the fixed rate will remain the same, which means that the total rise in your monthly or fortnightly payments will be lower than it would have been under a variable rate. Conversely, if the variable rates fall, you could find yourself paying a higher rate on the fixed portion of the loan.

Requirements of lending institutions

When you approach your bank or other lending institution for a loan, you should be aware that they have certain criteria that you must meet before they will offer you an investment loan. You may think that because you own your own home outright and have worked out that you can afford to borrow $500 000 to purchase an investment property in, say, Melbourne because the expected rent will cover your repayments, obtaining a loan will be a breeze. This is not so. The bank will require you to have an independent income, other than the weekly rent, to reassure them that you can still meet the repayments should the property fall vacant for a month or more each year. So an asset-rich retiree who owns a $1 million mansion, but has only a small retirement income, is unlikely to be given an investment loan.

As a conservative guide, most lenders will allow you to pay an amount equal to 40 per cent of your pre-tax income plus around 75 per cent of the projected annual rent from your investment property on repaying *all* your loans (house, car, etc.). Thus, if you earn $50 000 per year before tax and expect to collect $10 000 per year in rent, the lending institution is likely to allow you combined loan repayments of no more than $27 500 per annum, which is calculated like this:

$50 000 × 40%	= $20 000
$10 000 × 75%	= $7500
Total	$27 500

Be aware that if you have a credit card or department store card the lender will take these into account too, even if there is no money owing on them. Because you have the capacity to draw on these cards, your lender will assume that at some point in the future you will do so, and will reduce the amount of their investment loan offer to allow for payments on your cards.

Chapter 8

SELECTING A PROPERTY

Once you have decided on the type of investment property you wish to buy and in what area, and you know that you're able to arrange finance for a certain level of borrowing, it is nearly time to start looking at properties. However, before you start, you need to check out the rents being asked for similar properties in the area. This will allow you to calculate the likely return on your investment.

The rough formula I use is this:

Expected rental income per week multiplied by 52 (weeks per year)
Divide the answer by the purchase price of the property

As an example:

Expected weekly rent	$210 × 52 = $10 920 gross income per annum
Divided by purchase price	$180 000 = 6.06%

Personally, I am not interested in buying any property that is not going to return me at least 6 per cent per year from the outset (although the property climate in Melbourne and Sydney at the time of writing may not offer quite this return). However, you must look at the overall picture when deciding whether to buy or not because the initial per centage will rise as rents rise. If the area is set to boom or rents look certain to rise, a well-located property may well be worth purchasing even if it means riding out the first year or two of less attractive returns.

You are now ready to start looking for a property, so here is some useful advice.

Check out properties on the Internet

The Internet is a great tool for helping you find properties. I regularly check the websites of the real estate agents in my area, and have found some fabulous investment properties among those advertised. Two other sites I would recommend are www.realestate.com.au and www.property.com.au. Both sites allow you to select the area, price range and style of property you are looking for. At the press of the Enter button on your keyboard they will trawl the Internet and present you with details of all properties matching your specifications. Not all agents subscribe to both sites, so it is wise to check both. Some agents do not subscribe to these or other similar websites, but do have their own. Check out the newspaper advertisements of real estate agents in your preferred area, as they will probably list their website addresses there. You can then look them up on the Internet.

Using the Internet as a starting point for your search will save you a lot of time by bringing a whole bunch of properties from various agents together for you to consider. In addition, most of the advertisements will feature photographs of both the outside and inside of the properties on offer, so you will be able to see at a glance whether they are of interest to you. I particularly like sites that include a floor plan, as I can make an informed judgement straightaway as to whether the home is large enough to suit my profile.

From 10 potential properties found on the Internet, maybe only three will be of real interest to me. By viewing them in this way, however, I save myself the time and petrol required to drive to the other seven properties.

Many properties are open for inspection by appointment only. You make an appointment to view the property and the agent meets you on site to show it to you. Often you will be the only prospective buyer he is showing through at that particular time on that particular day.

The owners will no doubt have had a massive clean-up in advance of your visit in order to present the property in the best possible light and will be overexcited at the thought of a possible sale. You feel pressure to buy because the owners have put themselves out to allow you to see their home. You want to like the property before you even get there and may make an emotional decision to buy, even though the property is not quite what you want.

If you had viewed photographs of the property on the Internet and didn't like the look of the place, you could have saved everybody the time, pressure and false hope that inspection by appointment can bring.

Not all properties on an agent's books will be advertised on the Internet, as some agencies charge vendors to advertise their properties in this way. You should still check the real estate sections of your local newspapers, and look in the local agents' window displays. You should also telephone them and ask to register your details as an interested buyer.

Attend open inspections — the theatre of war!

So, you are ready to take the plunge, to lose your rookie status, to join the big boys. Your preapproved finance is burning a hole in your pocket and you are ready to sign on the dotted line. All you need to do is find the right property. It's time to start attending a few open inspections.

Attending an 'Open for Inspection' can be like entering into open warfare. The purchasing process is very likely going to entail a battle of wits between you, the vendor and the real estate agent. You don't want to end up with the wrong property, or even the right property at the wrong price, so you need to keep a cool head and plan your purchasing strategy carefully. Like all good generals, you are going to need a battle plan.

Check out the real estate advertisements in the local newspaper. Most newspapers have a set day or days of the week when they run a real estate feature, often in the form of a pull-out section. The agents know that this is the day when the greatest number of real estate buyers will be checking the paper, and will usually run a corporate advertisement detailing all the properties that will be open for inspection either that day or the next. For instance, a property that is going to be open for inspection on a Sunday may be advertised in the Saturday edition of the paper, as that is when the agent's corporate advertisement is set to appear, so check both days.

As you read through the advertisements, take a thick pen and circle all the ones that appeal to you. Once you have finished reading all the advertisements, take a pair of scissors and cut out all the advertisements that you have circled. Sort them into order of inspection time, and stick them on a large sheet of paper.

I find this method better than merely jotting down addresses, as you have all the pertinent details of each property at your fingertips — price, agent's phone number, features of the property — and you can appraise yourself of the relevant details as you pull up outside each property.

Take a copy of your wish list to each property inspection. When you get back to your car, having viewed the property, take a few moments to make some notes. Do this while the property is still fresh in your mind.

This step is especially important if you are viewing more than one property on the same day. After a while they all blend into one in your mind and, without written notes, you will be left wondering if it was the first property or the third which had the broken shower screen or the orange bedroom curtains. Both of these could be easily and inexpensively replaced, but imagine if you were to choose a property that had an old hot water system or a faulty air-conditioning unit. (In fact, I recommend switching such appliances on while you are at the open inspection to see if they work — you could be looking at big dollars down the track to fix them.)

You need to make an informed choice and to be aware that all additional costs need to be taken into consideration when formulating your offer on a property.

So, you are outside your first 'Open for Inspection'. Hunker down, and get ready to go over the top. You are now going to have to pit your wits against that most wily of individuals, your local real estate agent.

Dealing with real estate agents

There are good real estate agents and bad real estate

agents. By and large, they are a personable lot. That is because it is their job to be likeable.

If they can get you to like them, you will want to buy from them. If you want to buy from them, they are half-way to persuading you to sign a contract of sale, regardless of whether or not the property suits your carefully thought out investment profile. Remember, these guys are working for the vendor.

It is their job to sell; if they do not sell, they do not get paid. If you were in their situation, would you worry about whether the buyer is getting a good, average or, at worst, a bad investment?

I have heard it said that the most successful real estate agents operate on the premise of repeat business, and that it is not in their interest to sell you a dud property, other-wise you would not want to buy through them again. This may be partially true. I have certainly bought properties from agents who have been most helpful and I have always contacted them when I have been ready to make another purchase. Only once has any of them had a suitable prop-erty on their books for me to look at on the second occa-sion. However, the second time round, they have, without exception, all tried to talk me into purchasing a property totally unsuited to my investment profile, simply because it was on their books. So my belief is that the same agent can be either helpful or heartless — it all depends on whether you really want to buy what they really want to sell.

The odds are more likely that you will only purchase one property from any given agent, no matter how helpful they may have been the first time. By the time you come around to purchasing again, they could have moved inter-state, you could have moved interstate, they may have nothing to suit you on their books, you may wish to buy outside their area of operation — the variables are endless. While your friendly agent may well do their best to sell you exactly what you are looking for, in the end they are going to try and sell you whatever they have on their books — and the two are not necessarily the same thing.

The way an agent treats you is also an indication of the state of the market. I have bought when the market was stagnant, and most of the agents I met were helpful and courteous. They took my details and tried to match me up with properties that might suit. When they said they would phone me at a certain time, they would call exactly on time. I bought some excellent properties at good prices. I couldn't fault them. We were all happy.

On the other hand, around about that time, I had a friend who wanted to sell his property. His was a 1970s cream brick house, which had heaps of potential but certainly needed upgrading. As a bonus, it was in a good street in a desirable suburb. However, with so many houses on the market, the local real estate agents treated him with utter disdain. He received knock-backs from agents who did not want to represent him as his property was deemed too difficult to sell or because they felt he wanted too much money. In fact the real reason was that they did not have enough buyers and were only taking on properties which they felt they could sell easily and quickly.

I have also purchased when the market was enjoying a boom. Buyers were out in swarms and there were not enough properties to go around. At some open inspections the agent in attendance did not even acknowledge my existence. Others promised to phone me to discuss other properties on their books, but never did. I provided my details to dozens of agency offices, advising what I was looking for and emphasising that I would look at any property that came reasonably near the criteria on my list. No-one called.

My worst experience was making numerous unreturned phone calls to a certain agent in an attempt to view a property in which I was particularly interested. When I finally got through to the agent, I made an appointment to view it the next day. To get to the property on time, I had to leave work early and drive for 40 minutes. The agent didn't show up. The house was empty so I couldn't even knock on the door and advise the owner of the problems I was having in trying to view her property.

The next day I managed to track down the agent again. Her excuse was that she had forgotten to write our appointment in her diary. In any case, she had sold the house that morning. When I checked the sale price of the house the following month, using information provided by my local council, I discovered that it had sold for less than the price I had been willing to offer.

If you are setting out to buy a property and you are unsure whether it is a buyers' or a sellers' market, talk to a few real estate agents. You will soon work out whether the real estate cycle is enjoying a boom or suffering a bust by the way the majority of them treat you.

Ask questions

When you are viewing a property that you are interested in buying, make sure that you ask the real estate agent some questions. Find out if the vendor wants a short or long settlement, and if the asking price is negotiable. Find out why the vendor is moving — are they building a new home, upsizing, downgrading, or moving interstate? You don't have to pin the agent to the wall and interrogate them. Just a few friendly, but pertinent, questions as you wander around the property will suffice. By informing yourself as fully as possible of the circumstances of the vendor, you can formulate an offer that is of maximum appeal to them.

Once the agent realises that you are interested in buying the property, they are likely to ask you some questions too. This can be tricky, as you do not want to give too much away. For instance, they may ask you if you have finance already in place. You can comfortably tell them that you do: this shows that you are a serious buyer. Do not, however, tell them exactly how much you can afford. I will explain why.

Offering a property for sale in a price range, instead of at a fixed price, is becoming increasingly popular. In a rising market it is difficult for an agent to predict the top price a property might sell for. They could ask $180 000 but find, in four weeks time, when the property has not been sold, that similar properties are bringing $195 000. It is easier for the agent to market a house at a price range. The lowest price in the range is unlikely to secure the property, although the agent probably does not expect to get the highest price either. An offer by you in the middle of the price range, or above, is what they are looking for.

So, let us assume that you are looking at a property that has an asking price of between $180 000 and $200 000. The agent asks you how much you can afford to spend and you tell them $195 000. That agent is now going to try and talk you up to spending every cent of that $195 000. They are thinking of turning you upside down and shaking that money out of your very deep pockets. They will tell you they have other interested parties who are going to write up an offer tonight, or any other tall tale that is designed to scare you into making a high offer. Never forget that they are working for the vendor.

Another question that the agent is likely to ask is whether you are buying the property to live in, or as an investment. It is difficult to avoid answering a direct question like this but, if you can avoid answering it, do so. You could reply by saying 'I don't have a house to sell' as if you believe that was the reason for the question. Then jump in with a question of your own.

You may wonder why it matters if the agent knows you are looking for an investment property. In the majority of cases it probably doesn't. The reason I am shy of telling any agent too much about my reasons for buying is recounted below.

We were viewing a house in an up-and-coming area. It was close to a prestigious new college, a smart, modern shopping centre and public transport, and was in a very pretty street. The house itself was under 10 years old, it had built-in wardrobes in every bedroom, ducted air-conditioning, gas heating, a huge entertaining area at the back of the house, a garage and vertical blinds instead of curtains. In short, it pressed all my buttons. It was as close to our wish list as it was possible to get. We were sure that it would appreciate in value particularly well over time, as well as rent easily.

It was priced at what was at that time the optimum price for a house in that area. However, we had done our sums and it met all the criteria for a good investment. We weren't the only interested parties. A young, newly married couple was also at the inspection (I knew they were recently married as I had sneakily listened to their conversation with the real estate agent). They were very keen to purchase the house.

We went home and did our sums again. We were fairly sure that the other couple would offer the full asking price. We worked out that we could afford to offer the vendor $2000 more than the asking price and we would still be getting a good deal. We called the agent and made an appointment to write up a formal offer.

The agent assured us that our offer was an extremely good one. He also had a formal offer from the other buyers, but he was confident that ours would be accepted.

Later that evening he telephoned us to say that he was very sorry but the vendors had decided to accept the other offer. The agent could not understand it as the other offer was lower than ours, and the vendors had not even tried to get the other buyers to match our offer. (He was a very young agent and far more honest and forthcoming than any I have met since.)

The vendor's reason for selling to the other buyers was that they did not want their beloved first home to be rented out by investors. We had made the mistake of telling the agent that we wanted the property as an investment. He had passed on this information to the vendors, and it had worked against us.

So, always remember that every agent you meet is hoping that the contract of sale you will eventually sign is going to be for the house they are offering you and not the one the agent next door has on their books. Most agents will say anything to get you to make an offer. If you are not sure about a property and the agent tells you that they have other interested buyers, don't let that push you into making a rash decision. They may have other buyers; they may equally well be lying through their teeth in order to hurry you along. If you are interested in the property, what are you waiting for anyway?

Just make sure that when you do buy you are totally happy with the property you are purchasing. If it has most, preferably all, of the attributes on your wish list and if it is in a suburb you want to buy in and at a price you are comfortable with, then take a deep breath and make an offer.

Seeking help from a buyer's advocate

At this point, you may be committed to the idea of purchasing an investment property but be scratching your head and wondering where you are going to find the time to do all the necessary research, inspect properties and negotiate a fair price with the vendor. Relax! If you are time-poor you can engage the services of a buyer's advocate.

Also known as an adviser, a broker or a buyer's agent, a buyer's advocate will discuss with you the type of property that you wish to purchase and do all the research, inspections and negotiating for you. Naturally they will charge a fee, which will vary according to the scope of the work they perform for you. As a very rough guide, 1 per cent of the purchase price of the property is around the mark, although some companies offer a fixed fee. Many companies boast that their negotiating expertise should save you money off the cost of the property, thus paying for themselves. You may want them to do absolutely everything for you, from researching the area in which you are keen to buy, right through to finding the perfect property, or you may want to do a lot of the legwork yourself and just have the advocate negotiate the purchase price on your chosen property on your behalf.

A check of the Internet, using the key words 'buyer's advocate' and 'buyer's agent', throws up a host of companies that will undertake a range of such services for you. If you are not Internet savvy, check out the *Yellow Pages* under 'Real Estate Services'. Narrow your choice down to two or three advocates and interview them. Make sure that they have plenty of experience — former real estate agents often make good advocates — and ask them for examples of recent purchases they have made. As with everything else, the name of the game is to make an informed choice.

Chapter 9

CLOSING THE DEAL

Congratulations, you have found a property you wish to buy. Now it is time to negotiate a price and, hopefully, close the deal.

Making an offer

Unless you are buying at auction, you will need to make a formal written offer. If you are buying in a rising market where there are simply not enough properties to satisfy the huge number of potential buyers, you may only have one chance to put forward an offer. In this case, it is advisable to offer your best price straightaway. Trying to save a couple of thousand dollars does not justify losing a property that may have taken you weeks to track down. Getting a bargain is not what long-term real estate investment is all about: as long as you pay a reasonable market value for your property and the rent you receive for it meets, or exceeds, the 6 per cent return rule, you won't go far wrong. Over the next 10 years or so your property is likely to rise substantially in value, and you are going to be putting little or none of your own money into paying for it.

Conversely, if you are purchasing in a buyer's market, you may have the luxury of being able to offer and counter-offer on a property until you and the vendor reach an amicable agreement on price.

Do not waste your time with verbal offers. If you seriously want to buy a property, make an appointment with the agent to write up an offer. The offer should include any clauses you desire, such as 'subject to finance', and must clearly set out the amount of the deposit, the settlement date and the conditions of sale.

For instance, if the vendor has agreed to include their outdoor furniture in the sale, this must be clearly written into the contract. You will need to put up around 5 per cent of the purchase price as a deposit, to be held in the agent's trust account. The larger the deposit, the more serious your offer will appear to the vendor, which is why a minimum of 5 per cent is recommended. Your lender will provide the cheque for the deposit, and you have until the first day after the cooling-off period to present the cheque to the agent. You should never hand over the deposit to the vendor. If it is a private sale with no agent involved, give the cheque for the deposit to the vendor's conveyancer or solicitor. The deposit should be held in a trust account until settlement day.

Some buyers offer a cheque for the deposit at the time of writing up their offer, which can reassure the vendor that they are serious. However, until the vendor has accepted the offer and signed the contract, they have no legal obligation to accept this offer and may still choose to accept an offer from another buyer, in which case the deposit should be refunded in full.

Note: Cooling-off periods vary from state to state. Currently only three states in Australia offer buyers a cooling-off period. New South Wales gives five working days, South Australia allows two working days and Victoria gives three working days. However, legislation is changing all the time, so you should check the current cooling-off period in your state before you even start looking at properties. Asking the agent what the cooling-off period is when you are about to sign an offer may give him the impression that you are already thinking about cancelling it.

You should also be aware that once the vendor has accepted your offer and countersigned the contract, he may legally pursue you for 0.25 per cent of the purchase price of the property should you decide to implement your cooling-off rights.

Once the cooling-off rights have expired and any 'subject to' clauses in the contract have been satisfied, both you and the vendor are legally bound to carry through with the sale and purchase of the property. You are legally contracted to buy the property or be sued by the seller, and vice versa.

Importance of the conditions of purchase

The offer price and the size of the deposit are not the only factors that the vendor will take into account when deciding whether to accept your offer. The more conditions you put on your offer, the harder you make it for the vendor to accept it. For instance, if you ask for 90 days settlement when the vendor needs to sell in 30 days in order to avoid taking out bridging finance for the purchase of another property, your offer will immediately be less attractive. If you are purchasing for investment purposes, it is unlikely that you will be selling your existing home. The settlement period is generally only a sticking point when buyers need to sell their existing home in order to buy a new place to live in. They may put in a clause that the purchase will go ahead only when they find a buyer for their current property. This is very off-putting to the vendor who has no way of knowing if the property is likely to sell quickly. By putting such a clause in their offer, they are asking the vendor to tie his or her own fortune to theirs. Not an inviting thought.

As mentioned in Chapter 8, it is important to ask the agent why the owner is selling. Once you have this information, you can finalise your offer, using your knowledge to make it as attractive as possible to the vendor. For example, the vendor might be building a new home and need the money to pay for building costs. They might also be planning to rent somewhere while their new home is being built. You could add weight to your offer by offering to rent the property to them while their new home is being constructed. If you were to make the rent a little less than the market rate, even if only by $5 or $10 a week, you would be giving the vendor a powerful incentive to choose your offer over others they may be considering.

Another option would be to allow the vendor a long settlement period, say 90 or 120 days. This might be of interest, particularly if the vendor does not have a mortgage on the property, as they could continue to live there, negating the need to pay rent while their new home was being built. The benefit to the vendor would be knowing that the property had been sold and being able to stay there rent free. The advantage for you would be not having to meet your first mortgage payment until settlement day rolled around.

Once your offer is on the table, if the real estate agent flatters you and treats you like their best friend, it is usually a sign that the vendor is likely to accept your offer.

At the very least, the agent believes that it is close enough to warrant negotiating with their client and that a sale is likely to eventuate. Either way, they are mentally spending their commission cheque.

If they treat you with barely concealed contempt, you can be reasonably sure that they have a better offer and that you are unlikely to be breaking out the champagne later on that night to celebrate your purchase. Experienced agents may treat you with contempt even if your bid is the best on the table, just to frighten you into raising your offer.

The property inspection

Once you have made your offer and it has been accepted, but before the end of the cooling-off period (if you have one in your state or territory), organise an inspection of the property by a qualified building inspector. You may even make your offer 'subject to a satisfactory building report', but if there are other offers, this may make yours less attractive to the vendor. If you are buying at auction you will have to commission the report prior to the auction. If you later fail to obtain the property, or decide that you do not want it, the cost is not recoverable. The cost of a building inspection varies, but is usually between $500 and $1000 for a fairly detailed report.

The inspector will visit the property and prepare a written report for you, highlighting any problems. They should inspect the attic or under the roofline, and also underneath the house if it is raised on stumps. Their report should cover the state of the electrical wiring, whether the property has, or is at risk of, white ant (otherwise known as 'termite') activity, whether there is evidence of subsidence or water penetration, or any other matter pertaining to the building or the site.

If the report reveals an expensive problem to fix, such as termite activity, and you do not want to go to the expense of fixing the problem, you can call off the purchase. Your outlay may save you from a lot of future heartache, time and expenditure.

Buying at auction

Auctions have traditionally been the selling method for properties enjoying a unique advantage in the marketplace, for example, those with a water view that can never be built out or those situated on a huge block in an inner-city suburb. They are hard to put a value on, and so the agency recommends that they be put to auction and sold to the highest bidder. In a real estate market where prices are rising rapidly, as has been the case around Australia for the past two years, it is also difficult to predict how much the market is willing to pay even for an average property.

Nowadays, therefore, it is not uncommon to see auctions conducted on properties in fairly ordinary suburban streets. Either the agent doesn't know what value to put on the property, or the owners have been watching too many lifestyle shows on television and are convinced that they can get a fortune for their home.

To buy at auction, you should inspect the property prior to auction day and, if you intend to bid for it, organise a building inspection. You want to make sure that the property does not have any hidden problems (for example, it might be about to fall down!).

On the day, you should arrive just before the auction and wait for the bidding to start. The vendor will have been asked to set a reserve price, which is the lowest price they are willing to accept for the property. Only the vendor and their agent will know the reserve price. The auctioneer will start the process by inviting bids from the crowd. If the crowd is reluctant to start the bidding, the auctioneer may advise that he is going to make a bid, or suggest a price, to get things moving.

In some states it is perfectly legal for the vendor or their agent to plant a friend or colleague in the crowd to make dummy bids. As long as the bid does not go above the vendor's reserve, these bids are legal, even if they may seem rather underhand to you and me. They do have the effect of bringing out the genuine buyers, who will counterbid in response.

You are entitled to ask the auctioneer if the property is 'on the market'. The property is on the market once the reserve price has been reached. Once it is on the market, you know that any bid you make is possibly going to be accepted. If the bidding stops prior to the property going on the market, and you are the highest bidder, you will 'hold the bid' while the auctioneer confers with the vendor. They will be trying to establish if the vendor is willing to lower their reserve price. If the vendor agrees, the property will be declared on the market and you may find yourself the new owner of the property. But you may also find yourself entering into another round of bidding, as the person next to you realises that this is their last opportunity to buy the property.

If, on the other hand, the vendor refuses to lower his reserve price and there are no further bids, you (as the highest bidder) will be invited to negotiate with the vendor to see if you can reach an amicable agreement on a purchase price. If you cannot, the property will be passed in, and there will be no sale that day.

If you have successfully bid for a property and the hammer has fallen, you will be expected to sign the contract and provide a 10 per cent deposit immediately. Once you have signed, there is no cooling-off period and you cannot legally back out of purchasing the property.

In some ways, buying at auction is better than buying by private treaty. This is because you know exactly how much your rival buyers are willing to pay for the property and you only have to go $1 over their highest bid in order to secure the property.

However, the problem with auctions is that people often buy with their heart and not with their head. You may have carefully worked out that $200 000 is the top price you can afford to pay for the property to make your investment work, and that if the bidding is higher you are going to walk away. The man bidding next to you may also know that he can only comfortably afford to pay $200 000 for the property, but he is going to live in it. He has a wife and two little children who have already picked out their bedrooms and he is not going to let you beat him. He is quite likely to offer $210 000 just to get the property, telling himself in the excitement and pressure of the moment that he can always do overtime to cover the higher mortgage payments. In such circumstances, it is wise not to be drawn into a bidding war, otherwise you may end up paying too much for the property, thus reducing the return on your investment and being forced to meet more of the interest payments from your own pocket.

Whichever method is employed, negotiating the purchase price is a fine art — and never forget that an unscrupulous real estate agent is like a fox in a hen house. Just make sure that you're not the chicken!

Finalising the paperwork

Once you have agreed to purchase the property and your offer has been accepted, you will need to employ the services of a conveyancer, land broker or solicitor. The relevant professional varies according to which state or territory you are purchasing in. Basically their function is the same: to carry out title searches and prepare all the necessary paperwork to ensure that on settlement day the property is transferred into your name and you become the legal owner.

You will need to provide the lending institution, the conveyancer and the real estate agent with certain information in order for them to prepare the documentation. It is a good idea to type a list of the names, addresses and contact numbers of all relevant parties, and hand a copy to each of them.

It is also a good idea to request an inspection of the property a couple of days prior to settlement. You should check the house thoroughly and make sure that you are entirely happy with the condition in which it is being left. Check that the stove is clean (you don't want to have to clean it, do you?) and look behind the garden shed and/or garage. These are favourite places for vendors to put unwanted pieces of wood, flower pots, beer bottles and other junk that is too hard to get rid of or they have forgotten is there. Worse still, they know it is there but, for some reason, they think that you would like to have it!

Give the agent a list of any problems that you would like to see sorted out before you settle and ask him to make sure the vendor complies.

In extreme cases, you can instruct your land broker or conveyancer to withhold part of the settlement moneys until the problem has been fixed. Make sure that the agent knows that you are prepared to do this. The likelihood is that the vendor will get rid of the garden waste, or give the stove a good scrub, if he thinks it is going to affect settlement.

Typical contact list

Name of purchaser:	Jack and Jenny Brown
Address of purchaser:	25 Glenora Street, Highgate Hill 4101
Telephone:	3338 7776 (H) 3337 2276 (W)
Address of property:	2 Investment Street, Chermside 4032
Purchase price:	$200 000
Deposit:	$10 000
Settlement date:	1 May 2003
Conveyancer:	Chapman Conveyancers Address, telephone number, contact name
Bank:	Commonwealth Bank Address, telephone number, contact person
Real estate agent:	Joe Blow Real Estate Address, telephone number, contact person

Chapter 10

TAX MATTERS

Benefits of consulting an accountant

Before you take out a loan to purchase your investment property, be sure to talk to your accountant. If you don't have an accountant (I certainly didn't, believing they were only for rich people), get one fast. Your local real estate agent, or the property manager you intend to use, may be able to recommend an accountant who specialises in residential investment property. Or you can check out the *Yellow Pages* and choose one who advertises such services.

One of the many benefits of owning an investment property is that the Australian Taxation Office (ATO) allows you to claim a host of generous deductions every tax year. These can add up to many thousands of dollars per annum. However, the rules and regulations governing such deductions are extremely complex. If you engage the services of an accountant who specialises in preparing taxation returns for property investors, they will have the knowledge and experience to organise all legitimate deductions on your behalf — and the highest possible tax refund. They are therefore worth their proverbial weight in gold.

Structuring your loan to your advantage

Your accountant will also help you to structure your loan in such a way that best suits your circumstances. The purpose of the loan, and whether the property is purchased jointly or as an individual, can have a huge effect on how much the tax man gives you back at the end of each financial year.

Joint tenants

If you are purchasing the property as a couple, you will probably want to buy as joint tenants, which means that you both have a 50 per cent interest in the property for tax purposes. If one dies, their share of the property automatically reverts to the other.

Tax deductions and depreciation concessions will also be split equally. If only one of you is paying tax, or is paying a much lower rate than the other, the dollar return for the lower earning partner will be worth less than for the partner whose net taxable income falls in the higher tax bracket.

For instance, if you intend to negatively gear your investment and one of you earns $100 000 per year and the other earns $25 000, it may make financial sense to put the loan and the title deeds in the name of the higher earning partner. This is because, for the same amount of deductions, they will receive a larger tax refund at the end of the financial year (because they pay tax at a higher rate). Should the unthinkable happen and you and your partner later divorce, the court should treat the property as being jointly owned for the purposes of making a fair division of your assets. However, you may wish to have a separate document drawn up by a solicitor when you purchase your investment property, providing for the lower earning partner to be entitled to a half share in the property in the event of divorce or separation.

Conversely, if you intend to pay out your loan quickly, thus making the property income-producing in the early years of ownership, or if you plan to hold the property for only a few years and then sell it, you may wish to put your purchase and your loan in the name of the lower earning partner. This will have the effect of minimising any tax payable on the income, and the capital gains tax payable when the property is sold.

Your accountant can help you decide on the best strategy for your particular circumstances.

Incidentally, if you still have a mortgage on your own home, I would urge you to use any tax refunds to make lump sum payments off your mortgage, not your investment property loan. As explained previously, you are paying for your home mortgage with your own after-tax income and the interest is not tax deductible.

Tenants in common

The term, tenants in common, is used where two or more purchasers have an interest in the property. The shares in the property can be split in any proportion. Say yours is a syndicate of three partners: one partner may own a 30 per cent stake, another may own 50 per cent and you may own a 20 per cent stake. These proportions are also used for taxation purposes. If one partner dies, their share can be willed to whomever they wish, not necessarily one of the other partners.

Purpose of the loan

It is important when arranging your loan that you state

that it is for investment purposes. Loans taken out for investment purposes attract special concessions from the ATO. For example, you can claim all your mortgage interest as a tax deduction against your income. On a $200 000 loan at 7.5 per cent interest, that is a possible deduction of $15 000 a year. The deductibility of mortgage interest is entirely dependent on the use of the funds. Stating on your mortgage documents that the loan is for investment purposes removes any doubt as to whether you can legitimately claim a deduction for mortgage interest paid.

Benefits of consulting a quantity surveyor

Once you have engaged an accountant, and purchased a property, you may wish to employ the services of a quantity surveyor. Be sure to choose one who specialises in residential property.

Ask your quantity surveyor to inspect your property and prepare a construction cost write-off figure, if applicable. This will include an estimate of the original builder's construction costs — assuming the dwelling was built after July 1985 — plus the costs of any structural improvements completed after 26 February 1992.

As well as a schedule of construction costs (also known as capital works), your quantity surveyor can prepare a list of all the depreciable items that you can claim as deductions at tax time (such as carpets, blinds, tapware, built-in wardrobes, garden sprinkler systems, and so on).

Take the report they have prepared to your accountant. This will be a huge help to them in preparing your tax returns; it will also be a huge advantage to you, as a good quantity surveyor will find depreciable items that you would never have considered including in your tax return.

While it may seem like just another expense on top of all the costs associated with your property purchase, the returns to you over the ensuing years in the form of legitimate annual tax deductions should more than justify the fee paid to your quantity surveyor. Also, the fee for a quantity surveyor is tax deductible.

Please note that if you are audited by the ATO they will expect all deductions claimed for construction cost write-off to have been calculated by either a qualified quantity surveyor, the original builder of the home, or some other person qualified to make an accurate estimate of the building costs. They will generally not accept your own estimates. The ATO will, however, accept a reasonable estimate of the cost of plant, fixtures and fittings as calculated by you. The amount of depreciation is based on the actual purchase price of the item, or its current value if it is not new.

Can't afford a quantity surveyor?

If you truly don't want to pay for a quantity surveyor, here is what you can do. Firstly, you should ask the vendor for the name of the builder who built the property. You should also request that the vendor provide you with all receipts (or, at the very least, copies of such receipts) they have in relation to its construction. If you're very lucky, the vendor will have commissioned the construction, and will have the original receipts for the building costs. These will give you a good starting point.

However, if the vendor cannot assist by supplying the necessary paperwork, you should ring up the builder and ask them to provide you with details of the construction costs.

Note: it is the true cost of construction that the ATO is interested in, not the cost including the builder's profit, so be aware that this figure can be difficult to determine.

Do the same for any structural improvements that may have been made to the property post-1992. Let's assume that the property has a new paved driveway and a new galvanised garage with a concrete floor. Try and get receipts for the construction of these items from the vendor, or find out the name of the contractor that laid the driveway and built the garage, and obtain written estimates of the original costs from them.

I expect you are beginning to see that the cost of engaging a quantity surveyor is worth the expense. However, if you are good at detective work or if you are buying from a wonderful vendor who has kept every receipt, you can save yourself some money by doing this work yourself.

Next, you will have to prepare a depreciation schedule for all the fixtures and fittings in and around the property. You know all that junk mail that clogs up your letterbox? Well, now is the time to start collecting it. Use the brochures showing the current cost of items such as stoves, carpets, lino and so on to give you a starting point. Then calculate the value of similar items in your investment property. Remember, it is the current value of these items that you need to calculate, not their cost when new. As mentioned, this is one area where the ATO will accept a reasonable estimate prepared by you.

Allowable tax deductions
Most of the deductions permitted by the Australian

Taxation Office on investment properties have already been touched on briefly in this and previous chapters. Here we will go into them in a little more depth.

Construction cost write-off

As mentioned above, the age of the property you purchase is important. For properties commenced after July 1985 you can claim depreciation on the original construction cost (not to be confused with the purchase price, this is the cost of building the house, not including land). This figure refers to the cost to the builder, not including his profits.

For a brief period when this concession was first introduced, the deduction was 4 per cent per year for 25 years. This particular concession refers to properties for which building commenced between 18 July 1985 and 15 September 1987. The building is said to have commenced once the footings have been dug, although such deductions cannot begin to be claimed until the date the construction was completed. You should note that at the time of writing such properties are between 16 and 18 years old and so will attract only between seven and nine years of future deductions.

The write-off on a newer house, although less per centage-wise, is probably worth more in dollar terms, as newer houses generally cost more to construct and fit out (unless you bought a 15-year-old mansion!). After 15 September 1987, the construction cost write-off was set at 2.5 per cent for a period of 40 years from the date construction was completed. So, on a house for which construction begins today at a construction cost of $95 000, you can claim a tax deduction of $2 375 every year for 40 years. However, if you purchased a property in 2002

that had been built in 1995, then seven years of the construction cost write-off would have already elapsed and
you could not claim for this retrospectively. If a property
is purchased in joint names, the deduction is split evenly
between the purchasers.

Please note that this deduction is only available while a
property is being offered for rent. If you move into the
property yourself, all the tax concessions you have been
enjoying on the property will cease. If you rent it out later,
the concessions will again be claimable.

Purchasing costs

When you purchase a property, there are all manner of
costs payable in addition to the actual purchase price. As
discussed in Chapter 7, you will need to pay stamp duty,
conveyancer's fees, mortgage insurance, bank fees, and so
on. The government allows you to claim a tax deduction
for only some of these costs, namely the costs related to
borrowing — mortgage insurance, the bank application
fee, stamp duty on the mortgage documents and the like.
This claim is spread over a five-year period or the life of
the loan (for instance, were you to take out a loan over
three years, you would spread the deductions over the
same period).

Stamp duty on the cost of the property, conveyancer's
fees and other such fees are not deductible but are added
to the cost base of the property for capital gains purposes.

Non-cash depreciation

To give you an idea of what you can claim, listed below are
some of the items allowable as non-cash depreciation
deductions:

- carpets and other fixed floor coverings
- blinds and curtains
- built-in wardrobes
- heaters
- air-conditioners
- stoves, built-in ovens and range hoods
- above-ground swimming pools
- hot water service
- garbage compactors

If you are letting the property fully furnished, you can also claim depreciation on all household items that you supply for your tenant's use. These include, but are not restricted to:

- beds and bedding
- non-fitted wardrobes
- lounge suites
- tables and chairs
- microwaves
- refrigerators
- washing machines
- crockery and cutlery
- televisions and electric radios
- vacuum cleaners
- garbage bins
- lawn mowers.

The amount of depreciation, and the number of years for which it is claimable, varies tremendously, depending upon the item you are claiming.

You can visit the Australian Tax Office website at

www.ato.gov.au from which you can download their depreciation guides. But better still, relax, sit back with a nice glass of wine and a good book, and let your accountant worry about depreciation rates on your behalf.

Cash items

As well as the non-cash deductions listed above, you can claim a tax deduction for all cash paid out in relation to your investment property, with the exception of capital items (such as a new shed or carport). You must keep receipts for all payments, as these will be required by the ATO if they decide to conduct an audit of your books.

Such cash payments include:

- mortgage interest
- property manager's fees
- accountant's fee
- quantity surveyor's fee
- bank fees and charges
- building insurance
- landlord's property protection insurance
- water rates
- council rates
- emergency services and other levies on the property
- land tax
- maintenance and repairs on the property
- proportion of the cost of running your car (if you use it to collect the rent or carry out maintenance)
- proportion of the cost of running a home office
- cost of telephone calls and postage associated with managing your rental property

- strata fees (if you have a strata-titled property)
- strata insurance (if you have a strata-titled property).

Goods and Services Tax

As an average property investor who is not running a business or who is not otherwise registered for the Goods and Services Tax (GST), you can claim a tax deduction against all fees and costs associated with running your investment property, including your property manager's fees, letting and reletting fees, the cost of engaging a tradesperson to fix a maintenance problem, and so on. Deductions for such fees and costs are allowable in their entirety, including the GST component.

Capital improvements and repairs and maintenance

A capital improvement means the replacement of an item with one of better quality (for example, replacement of an old free-standing stove with a built-in stove, or a galvanised fence with a painted steel fence), or the addition of an amenity to the property (such as a garage). Costs for such improvements are not allowable as repairs. They are listed as capital improvements and their cost will be taken into account for Capital Gains Tax purposes (see section at the end of this chapter).

As a further example, if a property does not have a garden shed when you purchase it, and you later decide to install one, this is clearly an improvement. You will not be able to claim the cost of it as a repair or as maintenance. On the other hand, if the hot water service breaks down and a plumber fixes it by installing a new flow valve, this is clearly a repair and you can claim the cost of it as such.

The issue of repairs and improvements is one on which you will have to be guided by your accountant. The ATO does not allow you to claim the cost of a repair to an asset that was defective when you purchased the property, as it is deemed that you paid proportionately less for the property than you otherwise would have if the item had been in good order. For example, this condition might apply to the replacement of an air-conditioning unit that was old and only worked intermittently when you bought the property. If you were to repair or replace the unit within the first year or so of purchasing the property, the tax office would possibly disallow the claim.

Keeping records

With all the deductions available to you it makes sense to keep accurate records, so that at tax time you can ensure that you're making the maximum allowable claim. As we have several properties, we have a home office. Each property is given a separate drawer in a filing cabinet, and each drawer has several hanging files, the kind you see in offices everywhere. These are clearly labelled with such names as 'Letting Agreements', 'Insurance Policies', 'Purchasing Details', 'Council Rates', 'Property Inspection Reports'. You get the picture. All paperwork is filed away in an appropriate file as soon as it is received, so that this task never gets out of hand or becomes a chore.

When it comes time to file the year's tax return, it is a relatively simple matter for me to gather up each file and put the information in order. This saves our accountant having to do it, and saves us the cost of having him do it!

We have a computer at home and at the end of the financial year I prepare a spreadsheet for each property, showing the costs associated with running that property, to which I attach copies of all relevant receipts. A neat hand-written note would serve just as well. The spreadsheet includes details of all rental income and all outgoings, such as our property manager's fees, letting fees, council and water rates, repairs and maintenance, insurance policies, emergency services levies, postage, phone calls, car running expenses, advertising, revaluations, and anything else that can legitimately be claimed as an expense.

Our accountant already has a file that details all the depreciation costs associated with our properties. He only has to prepare a new one if we have purchased a new property during the current tax year, or if he has to add or amend some details (for example, if we had a concrete driveway laid at one of the properties to replace a gravel drive). This would be classed as an improvement and the cost would be added to the schedule for Capital Gains Tax purposes.

If we have purchased a new property during the tax year, I provide a file containing originals of all mortgage documentation, the Contract of Sale, the letting agreement (to show the date the property was let), the conveyancer's account, the quantity surveyor's report and invoice, any water rates or council rates paid upon acquisition of the property, and any other documentation relevant to the purchase and subsequent letting of the property.

This allows our accountant to set up a file for that property, prepare depreciation tables and keep records for possible future Capital Gain issues.

Once our accountant has all the necessary details, he requires a week or two to prepare tax returns on our behalf.

As my husband and I are joint owners of all our properties, all tax deductions are split evenly between us, and we each receive a return to check and sign. Once signed, they are returned to the accountant for electronic lodgement with the ATO. Our refund cheque is despatched quite quickly by the ATO, the accountant deducts his fee and sends us the balance, and we are ready to start again for another year.

Varying your PAYG withholding instalments

You should be aware that there is a form you or your accountant can complete, known as an NAT2036, which is basically an application to the ATO to vary the amount of your weekly or monthly PAYG (Pay As You Go) instalments. By estimating in advance how much your tax liabilities are likely to be, your PAYG contributions may be revised. So, as a salary or wage earner, instead of waiting until the end of the tax year to receive your tax refund, you will receive a tax reduction via your pay packet. Similarly, should you be self-employed or receive an income from some other source, you can use the above form to vary your PAYG tax instalments (previously known as provisional tax).

If you are incredibly self-disciplined, you may wish to apply for the NAT2036 and pay every cent of the extra money in your pay packet off your home mortgage (on which you get no tax concessions) regularly throughout the year. This is actually the most effective way of reducing your debt. However, most people are more likely to pay off a lump sum than a small weekly or monthly refund, as this can be so easily swallowed up by other demands. Please note also that if your calculations are not fairly accurate you could find yourself facing a large tax bill at the end of the financial year (although you can file this form more than once during the year should you realise that you have miscalculated your tax).

I would therefore urge you to consider waiting until the end of the financial year before making your claims.

If your financial situation is so tight that you are totally reliant on receiving an NAT2036 reduction just to meet the running costs on your investment, then you have probably overextended yourself. After all, if you are totally reliant on receiving, say, $75 a week to help you pay your regular outgoings, what are you going to do if you are suddenly faced with a $700 invoice for replacing a hot water system that wasn't working? Better to buy a less expensive property than risk getting into a financial mess.

Note: A new version of the ATO form for varying your PAYG (Pay As You Go) taxation payments is issued every year, in May. Applications made on old forms will not be accepted for processing. You must make a new claim every year. Copies of the correct forms can be obtained from the ATO or from their website. Check out www.assist.ato.gov.au for a guide to varying your withholding tax and a copy of the latest application form.

> As you can see, the whole issue of depreciation and tax deductions is a very complex one. If you are thinking of bypassing the cost of a good accountant and doing your tax return yourself, you could be making a big mistake — unless of course you *are* an accountant.

Negative gearing

When the costs of running a property exceed the income from renting the property, you are said to be negatively geared. Let's say you buy an investment property with an interest only loan of $220 000 and you rent it for $250 per week. The property brings in $13 000 per annum but costs, say, $19 000 per annum to run. You can claim the loss amount — in this case $6000. If you are an average wage earner on a marginal tax rate of 31.5 per cent (30 per cent plus the Medicare levy of 1.5 per cent), you will receive a tax refund of $1890. This effectively means that the property is costing you $79 per week ($6000–$1890 = $4110 per annum, or $79 per week) out of your own pocket.

However, add to this any non-cash deductions for construction cost write-off (say the property was built in 1999) plus depreciation on fixtures and fittings, and this might add a further $10 000 to your deductions, bringing your total tax refund to $5040. In such a case, you would still be negatively geared, as you incurred a loss of $6000, but the non-cash deductions would help bring this down to a real loss of $960 per year, or $18 per week. For $18 per week you get to own an appreciating asset currently worth $220 000.

If you earn a salary of over $62 501 per year, your marginal tax rate is 48.5 per cent (including the Medicare levy). For the same total deductions as above, your tax refund would be $7760. Add to this your rental income of $13 000 and you will see that your property is bringing in $20 760. As your cash outgoings are only $19 000, the property is producing a positive cash flow of $1760 per year, or $34 per week.

The second example used negative gearing to produce an after-tax positive cash flow. In a financial climate of low interest and lowered tax rates, the incentive merely to negatively gear and sustain a loss each year is somewhat reduced. However, negative gearing is still a sound strategy, especially in the early days of investment. How can putting a few dollars a week of your own money into an investment that has the potential to bring you tens, if not hundreds, of thousands of dollars of usable equity in the future not be a good thing?

The position you are aiming for, however, is a pre-tax positive cash flow where the rent you receive exceeds the cost of running your property — you are in effect receiving an income on which you must pay tax. If you have enough property, your rental income can replace your salary, and you can retire from the workforce and live off your rental earnings if you wish to do so.

As you can see, there are so many variables — the purchase price of the property, the amount of allowable cash and non-cash deductions, your individual tax bracket — that it is very difficult to work out the exact return on a property. However, you can see that structuring the purchase to suit your individual circumstances (by buying in the name of the person in the highest tax bracket, assuming that they are likely to stay in that bracket for the foreseeable future, to maximise your negative gearing claims) can make a big difference.

Selling your investment property — or not?

I would strongly urge you *never* to sell an investment property. The smartest property investors *never* sell. However, people do sell their investment properties all the time, and when they do they have to pay Capital Gains Tax.

Capital Gains Tax

This sounds ominous, but is not necessarily a huge cost. The capital gain is worked out by adding to the original purchase price of the property all purchasing costs (conveyancing, stamp duty, and so on), capital improvement outlay (for example, for a new shed or a new driveway) and all selling expenses (agent's fees, advertising, and so on). From this figure is deducted all the capital works deductions (such as any construction cost write-offs) and certain of the depreciation deductions you have claimed. This shows your total outlay for the property. The difference between this final figure and the selling price for the property is your capital gain. As long as you have owned and rented out the property for a full 12 months, Capital Gains Tax will be payable on only half the capital gain.

As an example, a property that originally cost $160 000 is held for three years. The purchase price plus all acquisition and disposal costs (see above), minus all the capital works and depreciation deductions you have claimed against the property while it was being rented, amount to a final cost base for capital gains purposes of $180 000. If the property is sold for $230 000, Capital Gains Tax is payable only on $25 000 (half of $50 000). Further, if the owner has no other taxable income for the year in which the property is sold, the capital gain will be subject to the usual tax-free threshold, currently $6000 (slightly higher for retired men over the age of 65, and women over 62). In this example, the whole tax-free threshold applies, and thus a further $6000 can be deducted from the capital gain figure, leaving just $19 000 on which Capital Gains Tax will be levied.

But remember, at the risk of stating the obvious, if you never sell your investment property, you will never have to pay Capital Gains Tax at all.

Chapter 11

PROPERTY MANAGEMENT

Choosing the right property manager

The cost of engaging a property manager is very small compared with the peace of mind they will bring you, provided that you take the time to check the agents in the area where your property is situated and choose one with a good reputation. You owe it to yourself to select an agent who is going to do their best for you.

Talk to two or three agents to find out what they are prepared to do for their fee. Ask them about their vacancy rate, current rents on their properties and the addresses of rental properties on their books. Drive past those properties and see for yourself if they are in a good state of repair.

Don't fall into the trap of thinking that the fee they ask is the only fee they will accept. Fees range from 6 to 10 per cent of the weekly rent, depending on the agent and the range of services they include. Some agents charge a statement fee of a few dollars a month; some do not. Some charge two weeks' rental income for finding a new tenant; some charge only one week's rent.

Compare the various fees and services offered by the agents and prepare to negotiate. The more properties you have, the more bargaining power you have, but it is always worth asking if they will lower their fee in order to gain your business, even if you have only one property.

You also need to find out how the property agent collects their rents. Do they expect tenants to go to their office with a cheque or cash every fortnight, or do they make it easy for tenants to keep up to date with their rent payments by offering direct debit facilities or Billpay/BPAY into their rental account?

Some of the larger agencies offer good tenant reward programs — tenants who pay on time and look after the owners' properties are eligible to win a small award each month, such as a gardening voucher. I'm not sure that these programs actually improve your chances of having a good tenant — I believe that people are either responsible or not — but they certainly don't do any harm!

Check whether the agent provides an end-of-year financial statement for you to submit to your accountant and whether it is provided as part of their service or as a chargeable extra.

Find out if they do quarterly inspections of their properties and send owners an itemised inspection summary. You may feel that such frequency is an intrusion on your tenant, but an awful lot can happen to your property in six months. Good tenants don't mind quarterly inspections. If they have rented for a long time they will be used to them and, besides, they give the tenant the opportunity to report — and the agent to notice — any niggling little maintenance problems that may need fixing.

Property managers can have all bills, such as water and council rates, sent direct to their offices and pay them for you out of your rental income. They can organise tradesmen, often at lower rates than you could negotiate for yourself, to repair and maintain your property.

Some agents will maintain a file of photographs of your

property, which can be extremely useful if you later need to prove that it was in a particular condition when a tenant moved in (in fact, if they don't offer this service, you should take photographs yourself).

Some agents will even prepare an itemised inventory of fixtures and fittings for your property, which you can use for calculating depreciation tables. If they do not offer this service, and you are not engaging the services of a quantity surveyor, you should prepare such a list yourself.

You should also be aware that most landlord protection insurance policies are only available to landlords who choose to have a registered property management agency look after their investment properties (see Chapter 13).

For the few dollars a week you spend on a property manager, the benefits are well worth it. A property manager is not a luxury, but an essential service. However, it is my belief that you should choose an agent who specialises in the area in which your property is located, as they will have a more accurate idea of your property's rental potential, and are well placed to carry out inspections and attend to any maintenance emergencies.

In fact, it's a good idea to put yourself in the shoes of a potential tenant. You are looking for a house to rent in a particular location. You will check the classified advertisements in your local newspaper and if you are computer savvy you may well check the Internet for property to rent. But if you intend calling a real estate agent to see if they have a suitable property on their books, which one would you call — an agent on the other side of town, or one in the area in which you want to live?

Local agents will often have a database of people looking for properties to rent in your area, so when your property comes up for renewal you may find that you won't need to advertise for a tenant. They are also in a position to screen potential tenants who call into the office to register with them.

Setting the rent

Once you have bought your investment property, you will have to negotiate a rental figure with prospective tenants, including periodic rent rises. Or you may have to come to an agreement on the rent and future increases with an existing long-term tenant. Could you do that? If not, then you have an even stronger case for engaging a property manager.

Many landlords become too friendly with their tenants and don't have the heart to put up the rent when review time comes around. Would you pay your friend $5 a week just so that they would remain your friend? I doubt it. But landlords who are afraid of upsetting their tenants by putting up the rent when it is warranted are doing just that. I respect all my tenants but I don't want to be their friend any more than they want to be mine, and to ensure it stays that way I employ a property manager.

Once you have engaged the services of a reliable property manager, you have to work out just how much you can reasonably ask for weekly rent.

This is an art in itself. Ask too much and you may find your property lying empty for weeks while you slowly persuade yourself that perhaps it is not as good as Buckingham Palace after all. On the other hand, you don't want to set your rent too low. When there is a glut of rental properties on the market, lowering your rent by $5 a week could well mean the difference between having a tenant and not having a tenant. However, let's face facts. You are in this to make your investment work for you, and you owe it to yourself to get the optimum rental for your property in relation to the current market.

When the rental market is tight and there are not enough rental properties to satisfy demand, tenants face intense competition and may miss out on several properties before they get around to viewing yours. You may therefore be tempted to push up the rent on your property to take advantage of this situation.

However, tenants usually have a good idea of what they can get for their money. Besides, no-one likes to feel that they are being ripped off. You may find someone willing to pay more than the property is worth just to have the security of a roof over their head, but you can be sure that the moment they move in they will be planning to find somewhere cheaper just as soon as they can. This could see you every year paying out the equivalent of two weeks' rent to your property manager to find you another tenant. It is cheaper to negotiate a fair and reasonable rent and, hopefully, attract a tenant happy enough to stay in your house for a long time.

The lesson is: don't be greedy!

Optimising rental return

If you have chosen the right type of property in the right location, and have presented it in excellent condition, then you can ask a premium rent. This is not to be confused with increasing the rent to take advantage of a tight market. A premium rent is one that is at the higher end of the market for your area, but is not so high that it puts off potential tenants. Tenants are happy to pay a premium rent for a premium property.

Just out of interest, if you pay $160 000 for a property that has a rental potential of $190 per week, you might think that if you had bought a property for $210 000 you would receive correspondingly more for it. You would probably get a little more, but it might only be an extra $15 or $20 a week. If you had paid twice as much for your property, you might still only receive around $260 a week for it. The price of a property is only very loosely linked to its potential rental return. This is why I have chosen properties in the average family home bracket and why I have chosen the best homes in this bracket. In my opinion, such properties consistently return the best dollar for dollar return, in terms of rental yield and capital growth.

When you were looking for your investment property, you hopefully studied the area in which you were interested to gauge the average weekly rental being asked for similar properties. This would have helped you set your maximum purchase price.

Now that you have purchased a property, prior to settlement, you should study your local newspaper's rental property classifieds. You have an idea of the average rent for the area, now you need to refine that information in order to decide on a rental figure for your property.

To help you do this, cut out the advertisements for similar properties in the area in which you have purchased, paste them in a notebook and ring the telephone number in each advertisement to find out the address of the properties. Then drive past them, noting their location, style and condition and making a note next to the relevant advertisement. Keep these notes and use them as a point of reference when you come to set the rent for your property.

In addition, note any properties that have been

advertised more than once. It may be that the landlord was not happy with the references of the first rental applicants and has decided to advertise again, but it is more likely that the rent being asked is too high for the area or for the condition of the property.

If your research shows that the property was in poor shape, you can establish also that it was probably not the rent but the condition of the property that was deterring potential tenants. If the property looked attractive from the outside, it is quite likely to be nice inside too. In this case, the landlord is probably asking a little too much for it.

You can see how you can use this information as a guide to the highest rental you can ask for your property. Checking out other investors' properties might seem like too much hard work at the time, but it could translate into dollars lost or gained when you come to set the rent for your own property.

Don't take too much notice of the projected rental figure quoted by the agent who sold you the property. They will either overestimate the expected rental return to make the property more attractive to you, or under-estimate the rental potential so you will not be knocking on their door down the track. By underestimating the rent that you can expect to get, they are safeguarding them-selves. In their eyes, the worst that may happen is that you will advertise the property for that figure and get it. On the other hand, you may see through their ruse and ask — and get — the proper level of rent that such a property com-mands. In that case, you will be patting yourself on the back because you are so much cleverer than the agent.

The figure to take notice of is the one quoted by your property manager. If they are totally familiar with the rents in your area, and if they keep up with the market and are aware when rents are rising and, on rare occasions, falling, they can advise you accordingly. With the information you have gathered from the newspaper advertisements in hand, you can sit down with your property manager and discuss what is a fair rent, both for you and for your tenant.

Preparing your property for rental

If it is at all possible, see if you can have access to your investment property prior to the settlement date. The vendor may be moving interstate and vacating the property prior to settlement, or the property may have been empty when you initially viewed it. You cannot legally back out of the purchase once the contract has been signed and any cooling-off period has passed, so the vendor will possibly have no objections to such a request.

By gaining access to the property early, you can ensure that it is looking its best when you or your property manager shows it to potential tenants. You will be able to mulch flowerbeds and cut lawns, so that the garden will look its most attractive, and clean down paintwork with sugar soap, water and a sponge. You will be amazed at the marks that sugar soap will remove from walls and painted doors. Make sure the carpets have been cleaned and smell fresh. Shower recesses, baths, sinks and toilets should all be gleaming. Don't forget the stove! If you forgot to insist on the vendor removing any old garden rubbish, this is the time for you to take it to the tip. A day or two spent cleaning up your investment property can translate into an extra $5, or even $10, a week for it.

If the vendor cannot allow you early access to the property, you may request to be allowed to show prospective tenants around the house prior to settlement day. If you build a clause to this effect into your offer at purchase time, you might run the risk of putting the vendor off your offer. However, if you ask after the offer has been accepted, they can only say no. You have nothing to lose.

If you cannot get early access to clean up or to show prospective tenants through the property (which would allow the chosen tenant to move in the day after settlement), resign yourself to having the property empty for a week while the agent finds you a tenant who can move in quickly.

Sometimes a prospective tenant will sign a lease on the property even if they cannot move in straightaway. It is worth it to them to secure the property and it is also of benefit to you, as you will be receiving rent even though the tenant has not moved in. You can use this time to prepare the property as described previously.

Even though it may not result in your receiving extra rent, it is still worth tidying up your property. There is a definite advantage in ensuring that the garden is clear of any rubbish, the exterior and interior of the house are clean, and all maintenance issues have been attended to prior to the tenant moving in. It is my belief that if a tenant moves into a property that appears well cared for they will be more likely to care for it themselves.

Make sure the tenant accompanies you or your property manager on an inspection when they first move into the property. Your manager should be able to provide a preprinted inspection form, and together they will note on the form the condition of all appliances and soft furnishings and the general condition of the property. Both will sign it, and each will keep a copy. When the tenant eventually moves out, there should be no arguments of the 'that garden rubbish was already there when I moved in' variety. You know that you cleaned up the property and, what is more, you have a signed inspection sheet to prove it.

Try and have your tenant move in on a Saturday or a Sunday. It may not matter initially, but most people like to move at the weekend. It saves them having to take time off work. When your tenant moves out, it will mean that their lease will expire on a Friday or a Saturday. Either way, subsequent tenants are almost guaranteed to be able to move in at the weekend.

Making drive-by inspections

I like to drive past our properties regularly. As mentioned above, if the outside of the house looks well cared for, then chances are the inside will be too. But even if you have an efficient property manager, nothing is a substitute for your own judgement.

For instance, if I noticed a car parked on the lawn of one of our properties, I would note that fact. If I drove past again in a couple of weeks and it was still there, I would phone my property manager and ask her to speak to the tenant. Cars parked on lawns not only look scruffy, but their weight compacts the lawn, their wheels churn up the grass in wet weather and, if parked in the same spot regularly, they can cause the lawn underneath to die off.

When the tenant leaves, you may well be able to take the cost of returfing or reseeding the lawn out of their bond, but do you want the hassle when a simple phone call could fix the situation before it becomes a problem?

Chapter 12

LETTING THE PROPERTY

Selecting the right tenant

If you have elected to appoint a property manager, they will find you prospective tenants by advertising your property, either in the local newspaper or via the Internet, and by attending to walk-in and telephone enquiries to their office.

They should keep you informed at all stages of the tenant selection process, advising you how many prospective tenants they have shown around your property and how many applications to rent the property they have received. You should ask them for feedback from the prospective tenants who have viewed your property, as this could assist you when you are looking for new properties to purchase or alert you to a problem with your existing rental property. For instance, you may be advised that two of the three people who inspected your property were not interested because it did not have any built-in wardrobes. From this information, you might consider installing built-ins in at least one bedroom to increase your property's appeal.

If you have not engaged a property manager and are showing the property to prospective tenants yourself, it will be up to you to extract this information. However, if the prospective tenant realises that you are the owner, they may be reluctant to give you an honest answer as to why they have rejected your property, as they may not wish to appear rude. Tenants have no such reservations when they are talking to an agent or property manager. Of course, if you have selected a good investment property, chances are that you will encounter few rejections.

Once your property manager has received one or more applications, they should talk to you about the quality of the applications. Remember, you only need one tenant. If you have only one application, but it is a good one, there is no need to advertise again. This may seem like commonsense, but some landlords will advertise again just so they have a selection of tenants from which to choose.

Let's say there are three applicants for your three-bedroom, 10-year-old investment property, which is situated in an attractive suburban housing estate. Your property manager will check out their references and report back to you. You can either let your property manager decide which tenant to take on your behalf, or you can be guided by their advice, but make your own selection. There is no right way to select a tenant: whichever method you employ, you are taking a calculated risk that the tenant chosen is going to be a good one. To protect you against the risk of making a bad choice, it is wise to take out landlord's property protection insurance, which is discussed in more detail in Chapter 13.

So why don't you have a go at deciding which of these three imaginary prospective tenants you would choose:

1. Jody is a single mother with two small girls and a cat. She works part-time and is in receipt of single parent

benefits. She has an excellent reference from the property manager employed by her former landlord, stating that she never missed a rental payment and the house was kept in tiptop order. She is only moving because her landlord has sold the house she was renting and the new owners have given her notice so that they can move into it themselves.

2. Phil and Amanda are a middle-aged couple with a teenage son, who have recently moved from another state. Phil has just started working in the area and Amanda is a homemaker. Their son has been enrolled at a school five minutes walk from your property. They have impeccable references from their church group and from Phil's former employer for whom he worked for many years. Previously they owned their own home, which they sold when they moved interstate, so they don't have any references from former landlords.

3. Kev and Joanne are a young couple in their mid-20s. Joanne works at an office a half-hour's drive from your property, and Kev works in a factory on the industrial estate 10 minutes down the freeway from the house. They are not married, and have just moved in together for the first time. Previously Joanne lived at home with her parents, while Kev rented a unit nearer to the city. His private landlord gave him a good reference.

Well, who did you choose?

I think all three applications have merit, but on reflection I would choose Jody. That is not to say that I would not rent to the other two applicants. Here is my reasoning.

Jody has two small children. She wants a permanent home for her family. She is in receipt of benefits, which means that she will most likely qualify for rental assistance from the local housing authority, making the payment of her rent not a problem. Indeed, according to the reference provided by her previous property manager, she was never late with her rental payments and always kept the house immaculate. She only moved because the landlord sold the property, so she is a long-term tenant. She has a cat. If she signs a pet bond agreeing to make good any damage the cat may cause while it is living on your property, this should not prove a problem.

While Jody may well find a new partner down the track and want to move to a new home with him, she is equally likely to stay in your house for some years to come. Maybe she will like living there so much she will apply for any new partner to live there too.

Phil and Amanda would very likely make good tenants. I like the fact that Phil has a stable work history, and that he and Amanda are active members of a church group. This reassures me that they are unlikely to start holding wild parties the day they move into my house. However, the only references they have are from their church group and Phil's former employer. These are both personal references, and what church group or employer when asked for a reference is going to give a bad one? Another worry is that they have moved from interstate. How long before they start missing family and friends, especially as Amanda does not work and will be stuck at home all day alone while Phil is at work and their son attends school. If that happens, will they decide to break their lease and move back to their home state?

Kev and Joanne might also make good tenants, but they would be my last choice. They are young and in love, and all is well with their world. Will they stay together? If they split up and Joanne returns to her parents' home, will Kev still want, or be able to afford, to rent the house? Kev previously rented a unit directly from his landlord. Can you trust the landlord's reference or is he only recommending Kev because he wants him to move out of his own property?

Was your reasoning similar to mine?

To allow or not to allow pets

One of the biggest dilemmas you, as a landlord, will face is whether to allow your tenants to keep a pet. As new landlords, we can think of lots of reasons why we should say no. Cats and dogs can stain the carpets; dogs can scratch the paintwork and the floor coverings and dig up the gardens, and their urine kills the grass. I could go on!

However, did you know that Australians enjoy the highest incidence of pet ownership in the world? Statistics posted on the Internet by PetNet (www.petnet.com.au) suggest that 64 per cent of the 6.8 million households in Australia own a pet, and 91 per cent of those report feeling 'very close' to their pet. Of those pets, 2.7 million are dogs and 1.8 million are cats, and 3.6 million households have a dog and a cat. A further 1.2 million of us (including me) have pet birds.

Of the Australians who don't currently own a pet, 53 per cent would like to do so in the future. Of all the tenants in Australia, and remember, there are almost 2 million of them, a significant number have or would like to have a pet. So, knowing that there are a lot of landlords who won't allow pets, why would you, as a tenant, want to move if you found a nice house to live in where you could have your beloved cat, dog, parrot or budgie living with you with your landlord's permission?

As a landlord who wants long-term tenants, my policy has always been to allow a pet, provided that the tenant signs a pet bond, which guarantees that they will be liable for the cost of fixing any damage caused to the property or the garden by their pet. I have not yet met a tenant who would not sign, nor have I encountered any significant problems caused by allowing a tenant to keep a pet.

However, each case must be assessed on its merits. I do not include 'Pets Allowed' in local newspaper advertisements for rental of my properties — I would probably be killed in the rush of applicants. Like any other landlord, I would prefer that my tenants did not have a pet. Why take the risk of an animal damaging your property when you do not have to? Nevertheless, I want my tenants to be happy living in my property, to make it their home, so I put as few lifestyle restrictions on them as possible. If they ask if they can keep a pet, I always look upon their application favourably. By looking after my tenants and being a caring landlord, it is my hope that they will choose to stay in my property for many years to come.

Having said all that, there are a couple of pets I would definitely not allow on my properties. They are rats and mice. I am sure they are delightful little creatures with huge personalities, but there is no denying that even in the cleanest environment they do smell. I have inspected properties for sale in which you can smell the 'mouse house' in the children's bedroom as soon as you step in the front door.

Signing the lease

Once you have selected a tenant and negotiated the amount of weekly rent, the length of the lease and whether they want to keep a pet at the property, both you and the tenant should sign a residential tenancy agreement. This sets out the exact terms you have agreed, including the date when the tenant can move in and the date by which they must have renegotiated an extension of the lease or moved out. It also states the agreed rent and the dates, or periods (fortnightly or weekly), when the rent must be paid.

Any special conditions for renting the property should also be listed. These may include the tenant agreeing to use a cutting board on kitchen bench tops and a grease drip tray under their car on the garage or carport floor, and not to make any nail holes or put adhesives or stickers onto the walls. Water usage should also be clearly defined. Commonly, the landlord pays the water rates and the tenant pays for any water used over and above the annual allowance set out by the local water authority.

The Real Estate Institute in your state should be able to provide a form detailing the rights and obligations of both the tenant and the landlord. A copy of this form should be provided to your tenant. In South Australia, for instance, a landlord or their agent must agree to give not less than seven days and not more than 14 days written notice that the landlord or their agent wishes to enter the premises for the purpose of an inspection.

If the rent is to be collected from the tenant's house, a prearranged date and time must be agreed to by both parties, but it must not be more than once a week.

When the property is about to be vacated by the tenant, the tenant must allow the owner or property manager to show prospective new tenants through the property a reasonable number of times, and at a reasonable hour, during the 28 days prior to their departure. This is to allow the landlord the opportunity to find a new tenant before the existing tenant moves out. (Often a tenant will move out on one day, and the new tenant will move in the following morning.)

Length of the lease

Leases are commonly entered into for a period of one year. Although some landlords lease their properties for six months, I prefer the agreement to be for at least one year. This is because the property manager charges the landlord a fee for finding a new tenant, usually the equivalent of two weeks rent. To execute a new lease for an existing tenant, the fee is quite often the equivalent of one week's rent. On top of this the landlord has to pay for any advertising of the property.

Let's say you have a choice of tenants, one of whom sounds attractive. Their references check out, but they only want to rent for six months. The other applicant on whom you are not quite so keen, but whose references also check out, wants to rent for one year. If you rent to the first tenant, you will effectively pay four weeks rental income to your property manager, as they will have to find you a new tenant when the current one moves out and will also charge you another letting fee. Such fees can run into hundreds of dollars. Suddenly, the second tenant becomes a more attractive prospect, don't you agree?

Some landlords think that by entering a lease for longer than one year they are unable to put up the rent until the end of the agreement. This is not so. You can put up the rent at any time if you give the tenant at least 60 days written notice (this may vary from state to state). I prefer to increase the rent only at the expiry of the lease, as long as the lease is for no longer than one year. If you have a prospective tenant whose references are good and who wants to sign up for a three-year lease, then do it. You can always write a clause into the agreement whereby the tenant agrees to a regular, prearranged rent rise.

One of the reasons a landlord may be reluctant to enter into a long-term lease with a tenant is because they know that a home with a tenant in it is more difficult to sell than one without. By entering into a long-term lease agreement the landlord knows that they are restricting their ability to sell the property. Most buyers, unless they are also investors, do not want to purchase a home with a tenant in it. They want to be able to move into the home themselves. I have heard of purchasers buying a tenanted property and then offering the tenant a cash incentive to move out, whereas landlords sometimes put up the rent in the hope that their tenant will decide to move out, and thus make it easier for them to sell the property.

Some buyers find it easier to reject a tenanted property in favour of one with vacant possession. On the other hand, an investor may be attracted to a property because it already has a good tenant, thus saving them the hassle of advertising for one.

Rental bond

When a tenant takes on a lease on a property, they have to pay a bond. If you have engaged a property manager, they will take care of this aspect for you. If you are collecting the rent yourself, you will have to obtain the necessary form from your state's residential rental bond authority.

The bond is usually equal to four weeks rent, and this money is lodged with the bond authority and held by them until the tenant moves out. The bond is in addition to the two weeks rent in advance that your tenant has to pay upon moving into your property.

At the end of the lease, unless the tenant signs up to renew the lease for a further period, they can apply to the rental bond authority to release the bond moneys. Both the landlord (or their agent) and the tenant have to sign a form to permit release of the bond moneys to the tenant.

At this point, if you believe that a tenant needs to make good any damage they have caused to your property, you can apply to the rental bond authority to deduct the cost of the damage from the amount of the bond. But it is important to be fair. You should not expect a tenant to pay for the cost of making good what is essentially normal wear and tear. You may well be justified, however, in asking for restitution for repair or replacement of a broken light fitting or damaged locks, or for professional cleaning of a large stain on the lounge room carpet made by the tenant. The bond moneys may also be forfeited, in whole or in part, if a tenant breaks a lease and skips town. The rules vary from state to state, but are broadly similar.

If you make a claim on the bond moneys and the tenant does not agree with your claim, the matter may be referred to the Residential Tenancy Tribunal. The tribunal will hear the details of the case, with both you and your tenant being given the opportunity to put forward your argument. The tribunal will then make a decision based on what they have heard. If your property manager attends the tribunal hearings on your behalf, they may charge you. Such fees are usually charged on an hourly basis and are usually around $50 per hour or part thereof. If you have a lot of properties in the care of your agent, you may be able to negotiate a reduced fee, or they may waive the fee altogether.

Chapter 13

LOOKING AFTER YOUR INVESTMENT

Maintenance

The whole issue of maintenance needs careful consideration when selecting an investment property. Are you handy around the house? Do you enjoy fixing things and running around the hardware shops searching for vital bits and pieces to repair household fixtures, such as a wardrobe sliding door? Are you able to replace the pads on the air-conditioning unit? Do you want to play a hands-on role in looking after your property? If you answered yes to all these questions, then I certainly recommend that you select a property within a reasonably short drive of your own home.

Perhaps it is your intention to let the professionals take care of your property. In this case you must be prepared to pay out more for maintenance in return for not having to spend your leisure time fixing up problems at your rental property while your friends are at home enjoying a relaxing barbecue or watching the footy finals. However, you will be able to select a property in what you feel is an up-and-coming area, regardless of its distance from your home, as you are unlikely to have to drive to it in the middle of the night to fix a leaking roof tile.

Whichever path you choose, all maintenance costs are tax deductible, both for the cost of the materials and for the labour. If you carry out all your own maintenance, you may choose to pay yourself an hourly rate to do so. However, you must keep proper records of all such payments and at tax time you must declare them as income. If you have a full-time job and are already claiming your maximum tax-free income threshold, it may not be worth your while to claim your labour. Your accountant can advise you on your personal situation.

An important thing to remember is that you must keep on top of maintenance issues. When your tenant reports a dripping tap or a broken latch on the mailbox, it might seem trivial to you, but ignore it at your peril. By not fixing such problems you are sending a clear message to your tenant that you do not care about them. If you do not care about your tenant's comfort, why should they care about your property?

You are also allowing your property to deteriorate. Two or three minor problems remaining unfixed each year will soon leave your property looking tired and run down. Such properties don't attract the best tenants, and before long the problems will compound. You will not be able to ask higher rents or attract good tenants, and your property will be worth less than it might have been if you had looked after it properly.

I have been lucky in that some of my tenants have been more than happy to carry out regular maintenance tasks for me. Although my property is an investment for me, it is their home, and they sometimes like to carry out small improvements to make it more comfortable. As long as tenants clearly understand that they need to seek the landlord's permission to make any changes, however minor, a relationship such as this between landlord and tenant can work very well for both parties.

I have always made it clear to my tenants that if they want new plants and mulch for garden beds, I will provide them, provided they undertake to plant them and spread the mulch. If a tenant were disabled or elderly, I would of course carry out these tasks myself. Many of my tenants have taken up these options, thus maintaining and improving my properties. A well-maintained and improved property can only increase in value. My tenants are happy because their home looks attractive, and I'm happy because my investment is being looked after.

I have had tenants ask if they can paint the interior of my property. Although this is rare as all my properties are well maintained, occasionally I have a long-term tenant who wants to paint the living room a different colour or put washable paint in the family room because they have small children. If I believe they are capable of doing a good job, I will provide the paint. If, however, I don't want the property painted for some reason — for example, because it does not need it and the tenant is on a short lease while their new home is being built — I have no difficulty saying no. Each request should be considered on its own merit.

Insurance

It is vitally important that you insure your investment.

Firstly, you need to purchase a building insurance policy for your investment property, effective from midnight on the last day of the cooling-off period (if your state has one) or in the case of auction, from the date of the auction. The property legally becomes your responsibility to insure as soon as contract negotiations have reached a point where you cannot legally back out of the purchase. This date is not the same as the settlement date, which may be some weeks later. Settlement is when your lender pays the seller's agent and the keys to the property are handed to you.

On the day of settlement of one of our properties, the driver of the removal truck hired by the vendor to move their furniture backed into the property's carport. Around $1000 damage was done. We had a tenant lined up to move in the next day.

Luckily the vendor still had building insurance on the property and he made a successful claim to have the damage rectified. If the owner had not had such insurance, we would have been able to claim on our building insurance policy, as we had taken one out on the property as soon as the cooling-off period had expired. As a further precaution, we instructed our land broker to withhold $5000 from the settlement price until the damage was rectified. This provided the vendor with a powerful incentive to make sure he filed his insurance claim and chased up the company to have the carport fixed promptly. As soon as the damage was rectified, our land broker released the $5000 to the vendor.

As well as the usual building insurance, which protects you against such calamities as your property being destroyed by fire (or damaged by removal trucks!) — and upon which your lending institution will insist — you can also purchase landlord's property protection insurance. Such a policy will cost you around $200 per year, depending on which state your investment property is situated in, and its value. Landlord's property protection insurance covers a whole raft of situations. For instance, a typical policy may pay your weekly rent and damages in the following situations:

- departure of your tenant without notice (up to six weeks)
- default by your tenant (up to 15 weeks)
- prevention of access (up to 52 weeks)
- denial of access by your tenant (up to 26 weeks)
- legal expenses (up to $5000)
- malicious damage or loss caused by your tenant (up to $50 000)
- property contents stolen or damaged by your tenant (up to $50 000)
- legal liability arising out of your responsibility as a property owner
- loss or damage to carpets, curtains, blinds and general household goods caused by fire, explosions, lightning, thunderbolts and earthquake (up to $50 000).

Individual policies will spell out their exact terms and sums insured.

Put yourself in this situation. Your investment property is destroyed by fire. Your building insurance policy pays for the cost of clearing the site and rebuilding the house. While this rebuilding is going on, the mortgage still has to be paid, but the house is uninhabitable so you cannot rent it out. If you have landlord's property protection insurance, the rent will continue to be paid for up to 52 weeks. It will also pay for the replacement of such items as curtains, carpets, blinds, light fittings, and other internal fixtures and fittings not covered by your building insurance policy.

If that is not enough to persuade you, then try this scenario. Your tenant falls over a loose paver in the driveway of your investment property. He breaks his leg so badly that he may never work again. He sues you. If you have landlord's property protection insurance you will be covered for public liability. Without it, you are looking at possible bankruptcy.

Landlord's property protection insurance is usually only available if you have your property managed by a registered property manager. This is because your insurer knows that the tenant will have been screened and that regular inspections of the property are taking place. This gives the insurer a safety net and makes a claim less likely than if you are renting out your property privately and collecting the rent yourself.

The landlord who lives in a different state from his investment property and rents it out without the assistance of a property manager is not likely to be keeping a close eye on his property and represents a poor insurance risk.

By insisting that you have a property manager, the insurers are guarding themselves against false claims being filed by unscrupulous landlords. A professional property manager is less likely to allow a claim to be filed if he thinks it is not warranted, and will certainly not file one if he believes the claim is completely false.

Policies vary in the amount of cover and the types of risk they will insure. Check various policies and choose the one you believe offers you the best protection. This will not necessarily be the least expensive, but who wants to save $20 a year only to find that they are not adequately covered when the time comes to make a claim?

Whenever I see one of those stories on a current affairs program highlighting the problems and financial disasters which have befallen some poor hapless landlord, even while having sympathy for them, I cannot help but question the situation.

The landlord is usually an extremely pleasant average wage-earner who had been hoping to help provide for his retirement by investing in a second home that he rents out himself without the benefit of a property manager. Straightaway this suggests to me that he was not making regular inspections of his property. A quarterly check of a property should be sufficient to show signs of any neglect and provide adequate warning to the landlord that all is not well.

Perhaps the landlord tried to gain access to the property but was denied entry by the tenant. This need not have been done in a confrontational way. The tenant only had to give a reasonable excuse as to why it was not convenient for the landlord to call on a particular day. Perhaps he had an unavoidable appointment and could not be home at the time the landlord had requested. The next suggested inspection time may have clashed with the tenant working interstate for a week, and naturally he would have liked to be home when the inspection took place. Both excuses sound feasible, don't they? But the tenant had been successful in putting the landlord off visiting the property without alerting him to the fact that there was a problem.

Such delaying tactics may discourage a timid landlord from pushing for an inspection. He may not have wanted to upset the tenant and run the risk of their moving out, leaving him with the hassle of reletting the property.

It is easy to let time slip away and before he knew it the best part of a year had passed before he decided to assert his right to inspect his property. A lot of damage can be inflicted on a house in a year.

Quite apart from a lack of inspections possibly failing to alert the landlord, the question that comes most readily to mind when I watch such accounts on television is why didn't the landlord have insurance? If he had approached an insurance company and been declined because he did not have a professional property manager and was therefore deemed to be an unacceptable risk, then surely this should have alerted him to the risk of managing the property himself?

For around $4 per week (less than the cost of an entry in the lottery) you can be covered against possible financial disaster — and the cost is tax deductible. Why wouldn't you insure?

Chapter 14

MAKING THE BEST USE OF YOUR EQUITY

As I have already said, I believe in never selling an investment property. The only exception would be a poorly performing property. But if you have done your homework and bought wisely, you should not find yourself in this situation.

I have lost count of the number of friends and acquaintances who have asked me if I intend to sell my properties and retire early. Why would I want to sell? Because you want to get your hands on some of that money, I hear you say.

So let's look at the following scenarios:

- My children are growing up and I want to send them to a private school. However, the fees are expensive and I will have school uniforms, sports equipment and books to purchase on top of those. I have an investment property that I purchased 10 years ago, which has doubled in value. I paid $150 000 for it and now it is worth $300 000. If I sold it and banked the money I would make, I could easily afford to send my children to the school of my choice. I would be investing in their education. Should I sell?

- My elderly parents have a number of maintenance problems with their old but beloved home. They are both retired and cannot afford the cost of renovations. It is going to cost around $30 000 to fix up their home. Should I sell and help out my parents whom I love dearly and who gave me every advantage when I was growing up?
- My husband and I have a dream. We want to travel the world. We have been to the travel agent and worked out that we would need $70 000 to allow us to live comfortably but not extravagantly as we fly around visiting different countries for a year. If we sold our investment property, we could afford to realise our dream. Should we sell?

I would not sell in any of these cases. Not because I am mean, but because there is another way of attaining my goals.

By visiting my mortgage lender and taking out a second mortgage on my investment property I could have the money I need without selling. The new loan would not attract tax concessions and deductions because it would not be for investment purposes. However, rents have risen since I first bought the property and the rental income will cover both the original loan and the new repayments. The money I borrow is not taxable as it is a loan and is therefore not classed as income. Of course, the weekly income I was previously enjoying from the property will now go towards paying off the new loan, but I have instead received a lump sum.

In another five years my investment property is likely to have gone up in value again. If I wished, I could draw down another loan. Perhaps I could use it to pay for belly dancing lessons and a trip down the Nile. The possibilities are endless.

In this book I have detailed the types of property on which my own portfolio is based. I believe that if you follow the same formula as I have done, you have a very good chance of making successful investments. You can adapt this formula to purchase units or townhouses, or executive properties in exclusive suburbs. As long as you research your market and make informed choices you are unlikely to go wrong.

I know you are both frightened and excited. I have been in exactly the same spot as you are now, wondering whether to buy or not to buy.

As long as you buy *something,* you will be heading in the right direction. If the rental income and taxation benefits cover the lion's share of the mortgage payments and running costs, so what if the property takes longer to gain in capital value? Maybe you might have made more money, more quickly, by following a different plan. But unless you buy a property — any property — you will never make anything at all.

The aim of this book is to help you, the Real Estate Rookie, to become a successful real estate investor. If you choose your first investment property wisely, you will hopefully find the whole process so enjoyable that you will be encouraged to buy another. And another! In just a few years you will have opportunities available to you that you never would have believed possible.

Should you retire early? Buy a Harley and ride around Australia? Send the children to a posh school? Help out your local church group with a donation? Think big! You could sell your existing home and borrow against one of your investment properties. By combining the proceeds, you could buy a home in the suburb of your choice!

Even if you only ever purchase one investment property, you will be doing far more than many of your contemporaries. Even one investment property can be used as a cash cow once the equity has built up sufficiently to allow you to borrow against it. If you make it a rule not to borrow too much or too frequently, you can end up with a seemingly endless supply of rainy day money.

Go ahead, get out the newspaper and turn to the Real Estate section. Become informed and get ready to transform *your* financial future.

Appendix

CASE STUDIES

The following case studies have been contributed by a range of investors and tenants from around Australia. I hope you will find them inspirational.

The viewpoints expressed are entirely their own and do not necessarily coincide with my point of view. Any property prices and rental values quoted in this Appendix should be checked with real estate agents or property managers in the relevant suburb or area, as they may not still be current.

Tim and Rachael, Adelaide, aged 32
Investors
Q. **Why did you decide to invest?**
A. We had repaid our mortgage and had no other financial commitments. We saw investing in property as a viable alternative to regular superannuation.
Q. **What made you choose property over other types of investment?**
A. We believe that property offers a secure investment with consistent growth. It provides us with a steady, regular income. It offers us the opportunity to self-manage and self-value our investments.

Q. **How many investment properties do you have?**

A. Four. We purchased our first investment property when we were both 26, and added to our portfolio at intervals of roughly six months. We are now 32 and our initial combined investments of $500 000 have already grown in value by just over 30 per cent.

Q. **What types of properties have you invested in and where are they situated?**

A. We prefer smaller homes, less than 10 years old, with small, easily maintained yards, that can be easily resold and offer a high rental yield. We currently own two three-bedroom courtyard homes, one two-bedroom villa and one three-bedroom Tuscan-style villa. Our properties are situated in the popular southern foothills outside Adelaide, in Coromandel Valley, Aberfoyle Park and Woodcroft, within 15 minutes drive of our own home.

Q. **What made you purchase more than one investment property?**

A. We wanted an investment plan that would create wealth for our future, and with finance relatively easy to obtain, it made property an easy choice for us.

Q. **Were you nervous when purchasing your first investment property?**

A. Yes, but foolishly we were reassured by a real estate agent that the house we had chosen was a good investment, so we went ahead. Our first purchase was a failure. We had not done enough research and we aimed too high. Our decision was guided by our hearts. However, we were not put off by this, and our next investments were better researched and, consequently, have performed better in terms of rentability, rental yield and capital growth.

Q. **What sort of rent returns do you enjoy from your properties?**

A. Our first house, a three-bedroom Tuscan villa in Aber-foyle Park, cost us $115 000 in 1999, and initially rented for $145 per week. It is now bringing in $190 per week. The next two were both purchased in 2001, in Woodcroft, which is a family-oriented, up-and-coming suburb. Both cost around $120 000 and returned $180 per week initially, although these have now risen to $185 and $190 respectively. Our last property was purchased in 2002 in Coromandel Valley for $145 000 and rented immediately for $190 per week. All the properties are in good locations, close to schools, shopping and transport.

Q. **How did you decide how much rent to ask?**

A. We did plenty of market research and we also took into account the advice of our property manager. You should not ask for too little rent. We find that a reasonable rent brings reasonable tenants.

Q. **What do you look for in a tenant?**

A. We are biased! We prefer mature people, employed, with no pets, and few if any children, with the intention to lease for long terms — and no shared households.

Q. **Have you ever had a 'problem' tenant, and how did you deal with the situation?**

A. Yes, but nothing too serious. One tenant moved out without giving notice, leaving some minor maintenance to be carried out and the garden in a less than satisfactory condition. We claimed the cost of repairs from the bond, and because of the time needed to put these things right the home took around 10 days to clean and relet. We also suffered ongoing disputes with one particular tenant over small issues such as poor television reception and who was responsible for cleaning the gutters.

Q. **You mentioned that you employ a property manager. Why not manage them yourselves?**

A. We prefer to employ a manager, for ease of rent collection and for initial tenant selection. A professional manager can ask more personal details of a prospective tenant and can conduct comprehensive rental history checks with previous property managers.

Q. **What do you look for in a property manager?**

A. Realistic fees, local knowledge, someone we feel we can trust to be on our side. We haven't found anyone like this just yet!

Q. **Are you glad you invested in property, or not?**

A. Yes, very glad. The capital gains have been fantastic, and the depreciation claims substantial.

Q. **Do you plan to buy more investment property?**

A. Yes, we are ready and waiting. We intend to purchase properties similar to our others, and in the same sorts of areas. We realise that we will have to pay at least $160 000 for something like this now.

Q. **What are your best tips for investing in property?**

A. Just do it! Don't buy with your emotions. Refinance, using equity from existing properties to invest in new ones. Have long-term plans. Get good taxation advice regarding the tools for investment. Research the market, and use the tactics that real estate agents use, i.e. don't be afraid to be pushy to get what you want. Have your investment loans preapproved before you go shopping. Check out independent lenders, not just your local bank. Check for the potential ROI (return on investment). Get to know other investors and learn their strategies. Everyone has at least one horror story, but only take notice of genuine investors who have had problems — everyone else has too much knowledge, but they're sceptics.

Annette, Darwin, aged 48

Investor

Q. **Do you have more than one investment property?**

A. Yes, I have two neighbouring units in a 15-unit block in Darwin. Each unit is spacious, open plan, and has two double bedrooms. The block itself is about 10 years old, and is three-storeyed rendered concrete with underground parking. Each unit has a balcony. The block has a mix of around 50 per cent rentals and 50 per cent owner-occupiers. I also own and rent out an industrial shed.

Q. **How old were you when you started investing in property?**

A. I began my investment strategy when I was in my late 20s and living in Queensland. I bought a block of land, which I later sold for a profit. I then bought a home to live in, and later, when I moved to Darwin, I bought a unit to live in. I made a profit on both homes when I sold them. Seven years ago I purchased my first investment unit, followed by the second one two years later.

Q. **Why did you decide to buy a second unit in the same block?**

A. The first unit rented well and had appreciated in value. When the second unit came up for sale two years later,

it was going for under the market rate. I knew it was a
good buy and so I purchased it.

Q. **Why did you decide to invest?**

A. I have always been attracted to the idea of being financially independent. My parents had a really good atti-
tude to money and taught me the value of saving and
building up a good credit rating.

Q. **What made you choose property over other types of
investment?**

A. Right from when I was in my teens I liked the idea of
owning property. It is security for me. There were no
government superannuation schemes when I first
started working, so I have always been conscious of
having to provide for my own future.

Q. **Were you nervous when buying your first investment
property?**

A. Not at all. As mentioned, I had already bought and
sold two homes that I had lived in, and had invested
previously in land. The idea of having an investment
loan did not worry me as I had done my sums and
knew I could afford it.

Q. **What made you choose your particular investment
properties?**

A. They are in a good area, are fairly new and are easily
rentable. Also, I did not want a property with a garden
that would need to be maintained.

Q. **How much did you pay for your investment
properties?**

A. I purchased the first unit in 1996, and paid $131 000.
The second unit was identical and came up for sale in
1998. I was offered it for $125 000, which was an

excellent price. Each unit is now worth $140 000.

Q. **Do you get a good rental return?**

A. The rental market tends to fluctuate a little in Darwin. The lowest weekly rent I have achieved has been $170 and the highest $200 per week, which I consider pretty good returns.

Q. **How did you decide how much rent to ask for when you let your first property?**

A. I checked the local papers and also consulted other investors in the same unit block to see what was achievable for the area and in the prevailing rental climate. I still use this method to determine the weekly rents.

Q. **What is the longest period either of your units has been vacant?**

A. I've never had a problem finding a good tenant, and two weeks was the longest one unit was without a tenant.

Q. **What do you look for in a tenant?**

A. They need to have a rental history that can be checked out and a good credit rating, and I also prefer to let to long-term tenants.

Q. **Do you have a property manager or do you manage the properties yourself?**

A. I employ a property manager.

Q. **Are you happy with your choice of property manager?**

A. My property manager is excellent. She is very thorough and keeps a close eye on my properties. She makes sure that the tenants do not fall behind in their rent. She also keeps me fully informed of everything that goes on with my properties.

Q. **What is your best tip for investing in property?**

A. Never rent to friends or relatives. If they get behind

with the rent, or fail to look after the property, it can spoil your relationship with them.

Q. **Are you glad you invested in property, or not?**

A. Very much. I will always have some security, something to fall back on.

Q. **Do you plan to buy any more investment property and, if so, where and what type?**

A. I expect I will buy more at some time. As well as the two units, I also have an industrial shed that I rent out, as mentioned, and I am considering buying another.

Lyndon, Gold Coast, aged 60

Investor

Q. **What attracted you to investing in residential property?**

A. My son got a job on the Gold Coast and gave me a good report on homes located near the beach, river and shops. I decided to purchase a property that I could rent to him. This would provide him with a nice home that he might not otherwise be able to afford, and would be tax effective for me.

Q. **Do you have more than one investment property?**

A. My son suggested that I think about buying another one in the same area. At the time, I was living in Adelaide, so I flew up to the Gold Coast and viewed about 12 properties, all in waterfront locations, and signed a contract to purchase one while I was up there.

Q. **Were you nervous about putting your money into property?**

A. No, I did not see how we could lose. My wife and I even borrowed all the purchasing costs.

Q. What styles are your rental properties?

A. The first was a three-bedroom brick home in a good location, which my son still rents from me. The second was a three-bedroom brick and timber home with a pool. My wife and I have now retired. We sold our home in Adelaide and now live in the second investment property.

Q. When did you purchase the properties?

A. We bought the first place in 2000. We paid $160 000 for it and rented it for $250 per week. The second house cost us $380 000 in 2001, and we rented it back to the vendor for $400 per week.

Q. Do you employ a property manager?

A. No! We had an investment property in Sydney, which we purchased in 1995. Due to an incompetent agent we had problems with the tenants and ended up selling the property. I have to say I think all property managers are useless, but what do you expect when you are only paying them $20 per week? Real estate people are like politicians, once they have your vote (rental) you never hear from them again!

Q. If your son moved out and you had to find another tenant, what sort of tenant would you look for?

A. A single mother, as they would be motivated to keep a roof over their children's heads.

Q. What is your best tip for investing in property?

A. Look after it yourself.

Q. Are you glad you invested in property?

A. Yes, yes, yes. We could retire only because of increases in our property values. Our house has increased from $380 000 to $670 000. Unbelievable — how could you earn that?

Denise, Melbourne, aged 42

Investor

Q. **What type of investment property do you own?**

A. A two-bedroom brick house at Patterson Lakes, with its own boat mooring.

Q. **What attracted you to property rather than other types of investment?**

A. I liked the security that property can offer, and I have knowledge of the property market.

Q. **Was it an easy decision to invest in property?**

A. I was nervous, as it is a lot of debt. However, I discussed the option with a number of other people who were knowledgeable in this area of investing.

Q. **Why did you decide to invest?**

A. To help save money for the future.

Q. **How old were you when you purchased your first investment property?**

A. It was 1987 and I was 27.

Q. **What made you choose your particular investment property?**

A. It was a combination of the purchase price and the possible growth in that particular area.

Q. **How did you set the weekly rental figure?**

A. I was guided by the rents being achieved for similar properties in the area. I also related it back to the purchase price, which was $113 000 in 1987. Initially the property brought in $110 per week, but is now achieving $280 per week.

Q. **Have you ever had a 'problem' tenant?**

A. Not really. Some tenants didn't care for the garden and some left it untidy. However, the rent was always paid. The property has never been vacant for more than two weeks.

Q. **I know that you manage your property yourself. What do you look for in a tenant?**

A. I prefer young families or mature couples who are financially secure.

Q. **What is your best tip for investing in property?**

A. Buy the worst house in the best street and the best location. You can increase the value by repairing or renovating the property.

Q. **Are you glad that you invested in property?**

A. Yes.

Q. **Will you purchase more investment property?**

A. Yes, hopefully in a more up-market area, or a property that would allow for development of units, for example.

Lesley and Geoff, Adelaide, aged 45

Investors

Q. **What attracted you to property as an investment?**

A. We had no superannuation or other retirement plan in place. We see property as much less volatile than other forms of investment, for instance the share market. Property investment allows you to have more personal control and input into your financial future, and is more visible. You can actually see what you are getting for your money.

Q. **When did you start your investment plan?**

A. We bought our first investment property in September 2000, when we were both 43.

Q. **What did you buy?**

A. Our first investment property was an average-sized,

three-bedroom, brick veneer home with a garden, in the relatively new suburb of Seaford Rise. It was a mortgagee-sale, so we were able to purchase it for $100 000, which was about 20 per cent under its true value, although it did need a little maintenance work done on it before we rented it out. We initially rented it for $140 per week, but this has steadily risen, and we currently get $160 per week for it.

Q. **Were you encouraged to purchase another investment property?**

A. Yes. We could not believe how easy the whole exercise was. There is minimal personal cost to investing in rental properties, and it was reasonably easy to get started. In February 2002 we purchased a second property, this time about 10 kilometres closer to Adelaide, in Reynella. Property prices had already risen considerably, and this time we paid $123 500 for a similar home, which we rented out immediately for $165 per week.

Q. **Were you nervous about investing in property?**

A. Yes! Before making our first purchase we talked extensively to other real estate investors, and asked lots of questions, until we had satisfied ourselves that we were making the right decision.

Q. **What made you choose your particular investment properties?**

A. We made a list of the criteria we thought a prospective tenant would be looking for. Our investment properties matched those criteria.

Q. **How did you arrive at the weekly rental figures?**

A. We checked the newspapers to ascertain the market rates for the area. We also reconciled the rent with our mortgage repayments to ensure that the rent covered our outgoings.

Q. **What do you look for in a tenant?**

A. We look for someone who wants a long-term tenancy. They must have a verifiable rental history. We also look for good housekeeping skills, which is something the previous landlord or agent will be able to comment on. We want someone who will take care of our property. Last, but not least, they must have the ability to make regular rent payments.

Q. **Do you employ a property manager?**

A. No, we manage our properties ourselves.

Q. **Do you plan to purchase more investment properties?**

A. Yes, something similar to our previous properties, and in our local area.

Q. **Are you glad you invested in property?**

A. Definitely, we had nothing to lose and everything to gain.

Q. **What are your best tips for investing in property?**

A. Avoid short-term leases. Before you make your purchase, check with your local council for information on any changes, upgrades or new construction/building works in the area that may adversely affect property prices in that street or suburb. Some changes may be beneficial, such as a new shopping centre being built nearby, or upgrades to public transport routes. You can also check with the local council for rateable values, local by-laws, and so on that might affect your decision to purchase. The Australian Bureau of Statistics can also provide information on median/average statistics for property size, location, prices, owner/occupier rates and so on.

Russell, Sydney, aged 45

Investor

Q. **What made you decide to invest in property?**

A. I'd tried investing in the share market and had been burned. I wanted the security of bricks and mortar, and was attracted to what I saw as a stable and growing property market. I see property as a secure investment.

Q. **How old were you when you started investing in property?**

A. I was 38. I was looking for financial security for the future and purchased a three-bedroom brick home in the Sydney suburb of Baulkham Hills. At the time it cost me $250 000 and I was able to rent it for $280 per week. It is now bringing in $430 per week, and has increased in value by 25 per cent.

Q. **Is this your only investment property?**

A. No. In 1999 I purchased a four-bedroom townhouse, again in Sydney, but this time in Castle Hill, for which I paid $315 000. The initial return was $440 per week, although this has now risen to $492 per week, with a capital gain of 30 per cent. Both properties have rented consistently. Neither has ever been vacant.

Q. **How did you decide on the weekly rents?**

A. I checked out the local areas and set the rent accordingly. Both homes are rented for the market price for their suburb.

Q. **What made you choose your particular investment properties?**

A. I researched the market and chose suburbs with good capital growth potential. I chose properties at the right price for the suburb. Both properties have enjoyed a healthy increase in value.

Q. **Have you ever had a 'problem' tenant?**

A. No, I've had excellent tenants.

Q. **Do you employ a property manager?**

A. I manage one property myself, but for the other I employ a property manager. I chose them because they could look after the property with minimal input from myself.

Q. **What is your best tip for investing in property?**

A. Buy in the right area, even if it is at the top of the market.

Q. **Are you glad you invested in property?**

A. Yes. I plan to purchase more, probably townhouses or semi-detached homes. I am considering purchasing interstate next.

George, Sydney, aged 44

Investor

Q. **How old were you when you started investing in property?**

A. I was 26, not long married, and the property was our first home. We didn't purchase it with the intention of renting it out, although later we did just that. The property was essentially an old mansion in Bondi, built in 1923, which had been converted to four townhouses. We bought one of the townhouses.

Q. **When and why did you buy a property specifically to rent out?**

A. We paid $68 000 for the townhouse in Bondi. That was in 1985, and by 1991 it had appreciated in value quite significantly. Because of the capital gain on our own home, we decided to purchase another property as an investment. This time the idea was to rent out the new property for a few years, and then move into it ourselves. We chose a period home in Ashfield.

However, our plans changed. We ended up keeping the Ashfield house purely as an investment, and bought a different home for ourselves to live in. We also kept the Bondi townhouse and rented that out for five years before selling it.

Q. **What made you choose property over other types of investment?**

A. We've also got shares. We play around with the share market and sell a few here and there, but basically we hold for the long term, the same as with our property, and we have experienced similar returns from both.

Q. **What is your current investment property like?**

A. It's a cottage-style, single-storeyed house in Ashfield, Sydney. It was built around 1910 and has two bedrooms, a lounge, a separate dining area, a sunroom at the back, and one bathroom. It's situated on a deep, narrow-fronted block, and has a lock-up garage at the rear, which is accessed via a laneway. The property is located in a relatively quiet street just off Ashfield's main arterial road, so the location doesn't attract too much traffic, yet it is only a 15 minute walk to Liverpool Road, making it handy to the shopping centre, railway station, schools, cafes and other amenities.

Q. **Were you nervous when buying your first investment property?**

A. No, not really. We looked at the history of our existing property, which had gone up in value significantly since we purchased it. We believed that if we chose the new property wisely we could enjoy a similar result.

Q. **What made you choose your particular investment property?**

A. The price attracted us. Our first home had been bought to live in, so we didn't really consider its investment potential, but with the Ashfield house we looked at price and a good location. At the time, similar properties in Bondi were selling for between $250 000 and $300 000 and we didn't want to pay that much. Ashfield is only 10 kilometres from the Sydney CBD and the area was up-and-coming at the time, so we figured it would be a good place to invest in. Over time, we have been proved right.

Q. **So you would say that both your properties have proved to be good investments?**

A. We paid $68 000 for the Bondi townhouse in 1985, and sold it in 1998 for $625 000. The Ashfield house cost $171 000 in 1991, and has recently been valued at between $550 000 and $600 000, so we believe they were both good investments.

Q. **What is the rental market like in Sydney?**

A. When we sold the Bondi townhouse, it was bringing in $380 per week. The Ashfield house started out at $210 per week, back in 1991, and got up as high as $350 per week a couple of years ago. However, the market changed and we had a period when it was vacant for four months. We held out for a while, but eventually decided to drop the rent significantly in order to attract a tenant. Currently it brings in $250 per week and is rented to a long-term tenant. Because of the capital gain we've made on the property we are not unhappy with this result.

Q. **How do you decide how much rent to ask?**

A. The market sets the rent. Basically, we follow the advice of our property manager. When we first started renting out our properties there was no shortage of tenants and people were willing to pay more than the advertised rent in order to secure the right property. To a certain extent those days have gone, although Bondi may be an exception because it is such a desirable location.

Q. **Have you ever had a 'problem' tenant?**

A. Yes. In Bondi, we rented to a couple who were sharing. They were struggling to pay the rent, which was at the market rate of $380 per week, and got behind on their payments. At the end of the day the agent resolved the problem and we eventually received the money owing. By coincidence, just at this time we were approached by someone who wanted to purchase the property. They made a very attractive offer and the tenants' lease was up, so we sold. However, we did not sell because of the problem with the tenants, but because the buyer's offer was too good to refuse.

Q. **What do you look for in a tenant?**

A. We leave the actual tenant selection entirely to our property manager's discretion. However, we do expect our tenants to have good, checkable references and we prefer long-term tenants. If a tenant wanted to sign a lease for longer than one year, we would be happy to enter into such an agreement.

Q. **What do you look for in a property manager?**

A. At the end of the day, we engaged the agency from which we purchased the property. We are very happy with them. Our original property manager left, but we are pleased with their replacement. We don't need the hassle of dealing direct with the tenant and the agent's fees are tax deductible. They can have the headaches. It's worth the small amount of money we pay them not to have to worry about it.

Q. **Your best tip for investing in property?**

A. The key is location. Wherever the property is, local or interstate, pick a good location and a quality property in reasonable condition, and make sure you check out the vacancy rates in the area before you buy. Adjoining suburbs can have very different vacancy rates.

Q. **Are you glad you invested in property, or not?**

A. Oh yes. It's quite obvious — when you look at the capital gains we've made. We're very happy.

Q. **Do you plan to buy any more investment property and, if so, where and what type?**

A. When prices settle down, we'll definitely buy more. You can only gear so much. We don't want to have to pay too much out of our own pocket, so we need to be sure that we can rent it out easily. With that in mind, we'll wait a while to see which way the market goes. Next time round we wouldn't mind purchasing interstate. St Kilda (Melbourne) appeals, as it's very trendy and the rental returns are better than those in Sydney at the moment.

Simon, Adelaide, aged 33

Tenant

Q. **What attracts you to renting instead of buying?**

A. I like the thought of being able to move at short notice if need be. I do plan to buy at some stage but I am not sure where I want to live or what sort of property I want to buy, so until then I'm sure I will continue to be happy to rent. Also, despite what many people say, it's not just as cheap to buy and pay a mortgage. I was a homeowner in the UK and know all the things you have to pay for as an owner that you don't as a tenant.

Q. **What do you look for in a rental property?**

A. I look for somewhere modern, clean and in a good area close to the city. I share with a flatmate so I look for a property that offers some privacy from the other.

Q. **What do you have to have in a property?**

A. I do look for cooling and heating, but that wouldn't stop me going for a place if it met my other requirements. Air-conditioning is something that some landlords will put in if they believe you are going to be a good tenant. Built-in wardrobes is something I always look for, and as I drive a company car off-street parking is a must.

Q. **What features would turn you off a property?**

A. Old houses don't interest me, as in the past I have found that things tend to go wrong and need fixing more often. I don't have a lot of time to maintain a garden, so I don't want a large grassed area with lots of plants and trees. Give me a small paved backyard with a few potted plants, so that I can sit outside and have a few beers with the boys and I'm happy.

Q. **If you found a property that really suited you and the landlord wanted to put up the rent at the end of the first year, how much extra would you be prepared to pay?**

A. My maximum would be $10 per week.

Q. **Would you look around for somewhere cheaper?**

A. If I really liked the place, I might consider paying more than $10 extra. I have found that if your landlord is happy with you as a tenant he would rather keep you than have to find someone else, so I would hope to come to an increase that we both agreed on.

Q. **In the Adelaide rental market, do you find it easy to find a suitable property to rent?**

A. There are a lot of places out there, but a lot of them are of a poor standard. Last time I looked (in 2002) I saw about 20 properties before I found one that was up to the standard I expect.

Q. **What type of property do you currently rent?**

A. I'm currently renting a three-bedroom, two-bathroom, split-level unit in Marryatville, with a garage, large living areas, air-conditioning, heating and built-in wardrobes. It's about 15 years old, and the weekly rent is $260.

Q. **If you moved again, what areas would attract you?**

A. I have lived in the eastern suburbs for around five years, and if I were to move again I would be looking for something in the same area.

Vicki and Mark, Brisbane, aged 47
Tenants

Q. **Where do you rent and who lives with you?**

A. We rent in Sunnybank Hills. We have two teenage children, plus two other teenage children who stay with us. We also have a poodle, three cats — and two lovebirds.

Q. **What attracted you to renting?**

A. We moved to Queensland as Mark had a job transfer from Alice Springs. We wanted to get to know the area before purchasing our own home.

Q. **Describe the house you rent.**

A. It has four bedrooms, a large kitchen, study, family room, lounge, dining room, two bathrooms, air-conditioning and a swimming pool. The location, Sunnybank Hills, is close to all amenities and public transport and has easy access to both the north and south coasts.

Q. **How much weekly rent do you pay?**

A. $280.

Q. **What was important to you when looking for a home to rent?**

A. It had to be large enough to accommodate all the family and it had to allow pets. It was important that it be close to public transport and amenities. Air-conditioning was a must-have, as were large living areas and lots of storage space.

Q. **What features would put you off a property?**

A. A small, dingy kitchen would definitely be out. We don't like dark houses, so it would have to have lots of windows and natural light. A small yard would be no good — we need a decent-sized yard for our pets.

Q. **You currently pay $280 a week. Would you be pre-pared to pay more if the landlord wanted to put up the rent at the end of your lease?**

A. The maximum we would pay would be an extra $10 a week. It would also depend on the circumstances — we don't intend to rent for long, but if we intended staying for a few years, we might be tempted to look for somewhere more reasonable.

Q. **Did you find that there were a lot of properties in the Brisbane rental market to choose from?**

A. Yes, we had no trouble finding something suitable.

Steve, Darwin, aged 40
Tenant

Q. **What attracts you to renting instead of buying a property?**

A. Never again will I owe money to a bank!

Q. **What do you look for in a rental property.**

A. Privacy. The location is important too. It must be close to where I work and within walking distance of my local pub, as I have an active social life.

Q. **Are there any absolute 'must have' features in your ideal rental property?**

A. None. I am fairly easy-going about the style, age and features of a property.

Q. **If you found a property that really suited you and the landlord wanted to put up the rent at the end of the first lease period, would you be prepared to consider a higher rent?**

A. Currently I pay $90 per week, which I consider fair. I would not be prepared to pay more, so if the landlord wanted to raise the rent I would look around for somewhere cheaper.

Q. **In the Darwin rental market, do you find it is easy to find a suitable property to rent?**

A. Not really. I just happened to be in the right place at the right time.

Q. **What type of home do you currently rent?**

A. It's a large, two-bedroom unit with a balcony, and the floors are tiled throughout. It is situated in Winnellie, which is an industrial area. It appealed to me because of its close proximity to my work.

Liz, Melbourne, aged 33
Tenant

Q. **What attracted you to renting instead of buying?**

A. My husband got a job transfer from Adelaide to Melbourne in 2001, and we decided to rent out our home in Adelaide and rent another for ourselves in Melbourne. We didn't want to buy straightaway as we didn't know which area we might eventually want to live in permanently.

Q. **Did you find it easy to locate a rental property?**

A. I looked up rental properties on the Internet and I also had a friend who was living in Melbourne look at places for me. I found one that sounded nice. However, when she inspected it for me, it was awful. I found another one, again on the Internet, and she looked at it for me and described it to me over the telephone. It was a larger home with a big yard (for the dog). My friend said that it seemed neat and clean, so I immediately rang the agent and said I wanted to rent it. We didn't even see the property till the day the removalist arrived. Apparently, on closer inspection, it had been quite dirty. However, I paid my friend to clean it, ready for our arrival from interstate.

Q. **Where do you rent?**

A. In Endeavour Hills, not far from Dandenong. The house has four bedrooms and two bathrooms. Endeavour Hills is in the Casey Council area, which is the fastest growing region in Melbourne. It's only 35 kilometres to the city, although the traffic congestion does mean that it can take an hour to get home from Melbourne in the rush hour. You can buy a huge home with four bedrooms in this area for around $200 000 to $260 000, and a lot of families are moving here because land is readily available.

My husband's sister rents a three-bedroom, one-bathroom house in Watsonia, which is only about 18 kilometres from the city, and pays $200 per week rent.

The houses there sell for around $280 000 to $350 000.

Q. **What do you look for in a rental property?**

A. As a tenant I look for space, because I have kids. I don't want a house on a busy road, and it must have a reasonable back yard. Now that we are settled in Melbourne, we are looking for somewhere else to rent, as this place does not have a lot of amenities that we now consider essential, having rented for a year.

Q. **What are the features in a rental property that are absolutely essential to you?**

A. The next place must have built-in cupboards as we don't have cupboards here, and heating is also a definite must-have. This house has no carport either, and it's quite annoying when your car is dirty five minutes after you've washed it. A lot of homes I have seen have alarms as well, although this one doesn't. Our current place has no shed or cover for our bikes, the barbecue, and so on, which is another annoyance. Neither does it have air-conditioning (although in Melbourne you probably don't need it). So basically I am going to look for a house that has all those facilities. It doesn't matter if it's smaller. I'll also be looking for a lower rent. Even if I can find another property at $10–15 cheaper per week that will be a big saving overall and we can use the money we save to invest.

Q. **What is the average rent for the area where you live?**

A. We currently pay $210 per week, although since we moved here we've found that rents in this area start at around $165 for something really small, and are about $185 for a three-bedroom home.

Q. **If you were to rent long term and found a house that**

really suited your requirements, would you be prepared to pay a little more for it?

A. Looking at the long term, as a tenant I would be annoyed if the landlord wanted to put up our rent by $10 per week at the end of each lease period. I might put up with it for a while but would probably start looking for a cheaper alternative. Maybe if it went up $5 a week I wouldn't complain, as long as the landlord looked after us and fixed things as needed.

On the flip side, if the rent was put up by $10 per week and I liked the house, and there were not many houses on the market (shortage of rentals), then I would be prepared to keep paying the additional rent. At the moment there is choice here in Melbourne — the competition is fierce. Just driving to the shops I pass about six houses that are available to rent.

Q. **Will you continue to rent?**

A. We are thinking of continuing to rent and using our savings to buy an investment property, as it would be tax effective for us.

Aubrey and Terryn, Adelaide, aged 30
Tenants

Q. **What attracts you to renting instead of buying?**

A. There are two reasons. When we first arrived in Adelaide 18 months ago, having emigrated from South Africa, we wanted to rent so that we could get to know Adelaide and decide which areas we liked before we made a decision on where to buy. Added to this, the costs of emigrating were high, so we were not in a position to put down a deposit on our own home, but we intend to do this in the future.

Q. **What did you look for in a rental property?**

A. When we first arrived in Australia, we had not rented before and did not know what to expect. We were definite that the house had to be clean and have a large, secure garden that would be suitable for our two young children to play in. We also wanted somewhere secure and under cover to keep our car. Later, having experienced an Adelaide summer, we realised that adequate cooling was also important — luckily the house we rent has ducted cooling. We also found that as we bought things like bicycles for the children and a lawnmower a shed is a big plus for storage. Having lots of cupboards in the house is also important to us.

Q. **What are absolute must-haves in a rental property?**

A. Good location — reasonably close to shops and the children's school, and not too far to drive to work. Our ideal rental would be in a quiet suburb, in a street where all the houses are neat and tidy. The garden should be reasonably large but low maintenance.

Q. **What features really turn you off a rental property?**

A. We would not rent near power lines or a busy or noisy road or a railway line. We don't like dark, gloomy houses, or loud colours on walls and carpets. We also dislike showers with 'chicken wire' screens that are prone to cracking. It is important to us that our neighbours' homes are also nice — we would not rent a nice home that was next door to a scruffy house.

Q. **If you found a property that really suited you and the landlord wanted to raise the weekly rent at the end of the lease period, would you be prepared to pay more or would you look around for something cheaper?**

A. We would not mind paying $10 a week extra, but if the house really suited us, we would be prepared to go up to an extra $20 a week. Having said that, if it became difficult for us to meet the rental payments we would look for something else.

Q. **What do you expect from your landlord?**

A. We expect to have any maintenance problems fixed within a reasonable period of time, no more than a week, or sooner if it is a big problem such as the air-conditioner not working.

Q. **Do you prefer to deal with an agent or direct with the landlord?**

A. We much prefer to deal with an agent. They are not emotionally attached to the property and we find it easier to discuss money or maintenance with a third party.

Q. **Describe the home you rent.**

A. It is a 10-year-old, three-bedroom, brick veneer house in a nice street in a fairly new suburb. It has heating, ducted cooling, a carport, shed and secure garden. It is clean and neat. It is cosy and feels like home.

Q. **What suburb do you rent in and how much is your weekly rent?**

A. We rent in Woodcroft and pay $185 per week.

Q. **Why did you choose that location?**

A. Not knowing Adelaide at all, the house could have been in any suburb as long as it was in the southern area, near to where Aubrey works.

Q. **In the Adelaide rental market did you find it easy to locate a suitable home to rent?**

A. There were a lot of homes on the market, and we looked at quite a few. However, hardly any were up to the standard or had the features we were looking for.

Louise, Melbourne, aged 30
Tenant

Q. Who lives in your rental property?

A. Myself and my husband.

Q. Are you intending to rent long term?

A. No, renting is transitional, while we save up for a deposit on our own home.

Q. What do you look for in a rental property?

A. It has to be close to the university and to work. It has to be clean, with a big fenced backyard, a good functional kitchen, a good oven (we like to cook) and a nice bathroom.

Q. What features would put you off renting a particular property?

A. I wouldn't want to rent on a busy road, or anywhere noisy. I would not want the neighbours to be too close. A smelly or dirty house would not get a second look.

Q. If you were happy in a rented property and the landlord wanted to raise the rent, how much would you be prepared to pay?

A. We would be prepared to pay between $10 and $20 extra per week. The cost involved in trying to find somewhere cheaper means that moving would not be worth it to us.

Q. Did you find it easy to find somewhere to rent in the Melbourne market?

A. Yes, it was very easy.

Q. What suburb do you live in?

A. We live in Watsonia. We chose this suburb as we

wanted to be close to the university.

Q. **How much rent do you pay per week?**

A. The rent is $200.

Q. **Describe the home you rent.**

A. It has three bedrooms and one bathroom. It has a modern kitchen with a dishwasher, a lounge, ducted heating, a wall air-conditioner, a secure, low-maintenance yard and undercover parking.

Richard, Sydney, aged 22

Tenant

Q. **What attracts you to renting instead of buying?**

A. I've got no up-front collateral, so really I have no choice at the moment, although I intend to buy in the future.

Q. **Where do you rent?**

A. The first place I rented was a two-bedroom unit in a block of 36 in North Ryde. I paid $270 per week, and stayed for nine months. Then due to personal contacts at work I managed to get a four-bedroom house, again in North Ryde. The house is about 30 years old, and I pay $320 per week.

Q. **If you were renting a property that really suited you and the landlord wanted to increase the rent at the end of the first year's lease, how much more would you be prepared to pay?**

A. It would depend on how much they wanted to increase it. I would certainly try and negotiate but, personally, if it was the right house for me, I would be prepared to pay up to $20 more per week.

Q. **In the Sydney rental market, do you find it is easy to find a suitable property to rent?**

A. It can take a little time to find the one you really want, and then sometimes it is not financially viable. Sydney does have a lot of rental homes available, but then it is a well-established city.

Q. **What do you look for in a rental property?**

A. Accessibility to public transport, views, proximity to restaurants and social venues, and minimal noise pollution from traffic.

Q. **What do you have to have from a rental property?**

A. I would like it to have heating and cooling, but this is not absolutely essential for me. A lot of rental properties in Sydney are quite old and they often don't have these features. I do like to have a garage or carport, or somewhere to put cars under cover.

Q. **What features really turn you off a property?**

A. Ugly decor, such as really dark walls and carpet. Dated decor isn't such a problem as you can ask permission to redecorate at your cost, and it's so much fun!

GLOSSARY OF REAL ESTATE INVESTMENT TERMS

Acceptance	Agreement to the terms of a contract or offer.
Adjustments	Moneys to be paid to the seller upon settlement for prepaid utilities, such as council or water rates.
Asset	Strictly speaking, an asset is something that produces an income, but the generally accepted meaning is something of value that you own (for example, a home, a car, money in the bank).
Bid	An amount of money offered for a property at auction.
Body corporate	The owners of a group of dwellings, such as units, townhouses or apartments, within a strata complex, formed to manage the units and areas common to the complex.
Bond	Usually four weeks rent, paid by the tenant in advance of a new lease and held in trust by the state's regulatory body, to be paid back when the tenant vacates the property, providing that the tenant has not damaged the property or defaulted on the rent.
Brick veneer house	A building or home constructed with a timber or steel frame and a single skin of brick.
Bridging finance	A short-term loan, taken out to provide finance for the purchase of a

	new home when the buyer's old home has not yet been sold.
Building insurance	Insurance that covers the building, fixtures and fittings.
Capital gain	Profit made when an asset is sold.
Capital Gains Tax	A tax payable on the profit made when an investment asset is sold, providing that the asset was purchased after September 1985. Capital Gains Tax is not payable on the profit made on the sale of a residential property that is a person's main place of residence.
Capped loan	Similar to a fixed rate loan except that the rate may fall below, but cannot rise above, the capped level.
Certificate of title	A document issued by the registrar of the Titles Office detailing the land dimensions and ownership details of a property. It also shows whether there are any encumbrances.
Common property	The common areas of a strata complex, such as the garden, pool and walkways, owned and used by all the tenants in common.
Community title	In many ways similar to strata title, the individual unit owners own a share of the common property but hold Torrens title over their own dwelling.
Company title	A title signifying that a complex of units or flats is owned by a company, the shareholders of which are the owners of the individual units. Individual dwellings may not be sold without the permission of the majority of the other shareholders.

Construction cost	A legitimate tax deduction write-off based on the construction cost of a property built after July 1985.
Contract of sale	The written agreement, signed by buyer and seller, in which the terms and conditions of the sale and purchase of a particular property are agreed (known as an offer and acceptance in Western Australia).
Conveyancer	Also called a land broker, this is a person or company registered to prepare and complete all the necessary paperwork to ensure the legal transfer of a property title from the seller to the buyer. In some states a solicitor would carry out this task.
Cooling-off period	Currently only applicable in three states, this refers to the period of time after a contract has been signed by both buyer and seller during which the buyer may cancel the contract. In New South Wales it is five clear working days, in South Australia it is only two clear working days and in Victoria it is three working days.
Deed	Legal document recording all transactions relating to the sale and purchase of a property.
Deposit	A sum of money paid by the buyer of a property at the end of the cooling-off period, usually 5–10 per cent of the purchase price, and held in trust by the real estate agent until the settlement date.
Depreciation	A tax deduction based on the cost and life expectancy of a fixture or fitting.
Dummy bid	A false bid made at auction by, or on

behalf of, the vendor, intended to stimulate the bidding.

Easement

A piece of land, clearly marked in the title plans, for which the council or some other body retains the right of clear passage. Usually this means that this part of the block of land cannot be built on in case access is required, for example, to repair water pipes underneath the surface of the land.

Encumbrance

A charge or outstanding debt on a property.

Equity

Per centage or cash amount of a property or asset that is owned free of debt.

Equity loan

A loan or mortgage secured by your own home, or other substantial asset, in which you have built up equity.

Establishment fee

Amount sometimes charged by a bank or other lender to set up a mortgage

Exchange of contracts

The point at which the buyer and the seller legally enter into a contract, both parties retaining a copy of the documentation.

Fittings

Items that can be removed from a property without damaging it, which may or may not remain in place when the property is sold. Examples are light fittings, ceiling fans, dishwasher.

Fixed interest loan

A loan where the rate of interest is fixed at an agreed level for an agreed period (usually between one and five years).

Freehold

Property owned indefinitely, as opposed to leasehold.

Gazumping

Refers to a seller accepting a higher offer for a property from a buyer after

	verbally agreeing to another buyer's offer.
Gearing	As in positive or negative gearing, this is the ratio of your own money in relation to mortgage or loan funds in an investment.
Inclusions	Fittings agreed to be included on sale of a property.
Interest	Amount of money charged by a bank or lending institution on top of the actual moneys borrowed.
Interest only loan	A mortgage or loan where only the interest, and none of the principal, is paid over the term of the loan; the whole of the principal is paid back at the end of the term of the loan.
Investment loan	A mortgage or loan taken out specifically for investment purposes, usually secured against your own home plus the investment property.
Joint tenants	The parties named on the title deeds as jointly owning a property; if one party dies their share reverts automatically to the surviving party.
Land broker	See *Conveyancer.*
Landlord's property insurance	An insurance policy that protects the landlord against loss of rent, wilful or accidental damage by a tenant, and other calamities.
Land tax	A tax charged by the state government on the land component of a property (usually other than your principal place of residence).
Lease	A legally enforceable document, which grants a person the tenancy of a property for a specific term.

Leasehold	Where a property is leased for a set period, say 50 years, for a set sum of money. When the lease expires, possession of the property reverts to the owner.
Lessee	The tenant or person leasing a property.
Lessor	The legal owner of a property.
Liabilities	Legal obligations and debts.
LVR	Loan to valuation ratio — most lenders will lend up to 80 per cent of the value of a property without requiring mortgage insurance.
Median rent	The median is the middle number in an ordered sequence of numbers, arranged in order of size — largest to smallest. Thus, in a study of weekly rents in a suburb comprising 97 rental houses, the median rent would be represented by the rent for the house precisely in the middle of the sequence, regardless of how little rent those below might attract, or how high the rents for those above it might be.
Mortgage	Security for a loan to buy a property. If the borrower defaults on mortgage payments, the lender can take over the property and sell it to recover their costs.
Mortgagee	The lender.
Mortgage insurance	Insurance paid by the borrower to protect the lender should the borrower default on loan payments.
Mortgage stamp	A tax levied by the state government based on the amount of mortgage moneys borrowed.

Mortgagor	The borrower.
Negative gearing	A legitimate tax advantage available to an owner of an investment property when the return on an investment does not cover the cost of the investment.
Non-cash deductions	Tax deductions allowed against income for construction cost write-offs and depreciation of plant, fixtures and fittings.
Offer to purchase	A legal written offer from a buyer to purchase a property at an amount and under terms specified in the offer.
On the market	At auction, when bidding for a property reaches the reserve price set by the vendor, the property is said to be 'on the market' and will be sold to the highest bidder.
Passed in	When none of the bids at an auction are accepted by the seller and the property fails to meet the reserve, it is deemed 'passed in'.
PAYG	Pay As You Go — a method of collecting taxes from a worker's weekly or monthly pay packet.
Preapproved loan	An agreement by a lending institution, prior to your finding a property, to lend you up to a certain level of funding.
Principal	The sum borrowed, on which interest is payable.
Principal and interest loan	A loan under which a borrower pays off the interest and a portion of the principal at an agreed rate.
Private sale	A sale of property for which the vendor does not engage the services of a real estate agent.

Private treaty	The usual method of sale for a residential property, as opposed to buying at auction.
Purpose of loan	The purpose of the loan must be stated when borrowing money to fund an investment, otherwise any taxation benefits will be adversely affected.
Quiet enjoyment	A tenant is entitled to 'quiet enjoyment' of a property, with no interference from the landlord.
Rateable values	The value the local council assigns to a property, regardless of the actual market value of the home. The council then charges a set rate, say 0.005 for every dollar of rateable value, for council rates. On a $150 000 rateable value at 0.005 the annual rates due would be $850.
Redraw facility	A facility provided on some loans, which allows the borrower to redraw funds that have been paid over and above the amount due.
Refinance	A property is refinanced when a borrower takes out a new loan, either from the original lender or another, and pays out the original loan.
Reserve	Prior to a sale by auction, the vendor agrees a 'reserve', which is the lowest price they will accept for the property. Once the reserve price has been reached, the property will be sold to the highest bidder. If the reserve is not met, the seller can legally withdraw the property from sale.
Residential tenancy agreement	A residential tenancy agreement allows a tenant to take 'possession' of a property for a limited period of time

on certain conditions, including the payment of rent. The residential tenancy agreement is a legally binding contract whereby both parties agree to abide by the conditions set out in the agreement.

Residential tenancy tribunal
State-run tribunal which decides the outcome of disputes between landlords and tenants.

ROI
Return on investment.

Security
An asset that is used to secure a loan. If the borrower defaults on payments, the asset can be sold to allow the lender to recover the amount owing.

Settlement date
The date on which all payments are exchanged and the buyer takes legal possession of the property.

Split loan
A loan where the interest is fixed on an agreed portion of the loan and variable on the remaining portion, for example, 40 per cent fixed, 60 per cent variable.

Stamp duty
A state government tax based on the purchase price of a property, payable by the buyer.

Strata title
Ownership of an individual dwelling within a larger complex (for example, a block of apartments or units). The common, shared areas of the property within the complex are jointly owned by each unit holder via a body corporate.

Stratum title
The same as strata title, with the important distinction that owners of the individual dwellings become shareholders in the company that manages the common areas.

Survey	A plan or blueprint that sets out the boundaries of a block of land and the position of any buildings on it.
Tenants in common	Term applied when two or more persons purchase a property and ownership is divided between them at a preagreed per centage. If one person dies, their estate can be left to a person of their choosing, not necessarily the other owners of the property.
Term	Agreed length of a loan, say 20 years.
Title search	Process undertaken at the Land Titles Office to ensure ownership of a property.
Torrens title	The legal documentation that records the owner of a property. Title in the property remains with the owner until they choose to sell it.
Townhouse	Usually two or more two-storeyed dwellings joined in some way, sometimes by common walls, often by garages. Most often these are strata titled.
Transfer	The legal document used to transfer ownership when a property is sold. It is recorded and held at the Land Titles Office.
Unencumbered	Owned free and clear of all debt and liability.
Valuation	A report by a licensed valuer, usually paid for by the borrower but commissioned by the lender, stating the perceived value of a property. This value may differ from the agreed purchase price.
Variable interest	Per centage rate of interest charged on

	loan funds, which varies up or down over the life of the loan.
Vendor	The seller.
Vendor bid	A bid made on behalf of the vendor at auction, and declared as such by the auctioneer; often used to start the bidding if no other bids have been made.
Yield	Rental income from a property expressed as a per centage of the purchase price.
Zoning	Permitted use of land as established by the local authority — for example, if a property or block is zoned 'industrial', residential building will not be permitted.

INDEX

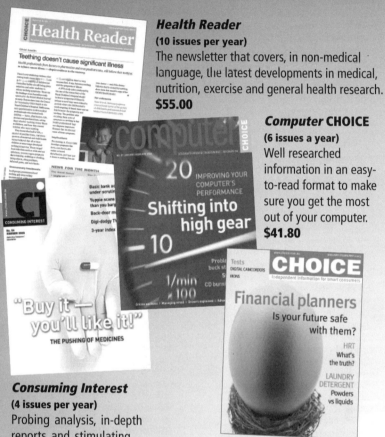